The Soul Garden Within

The Soul Garden Within

Growing Spiritual Consciousness

Sally Gallot-Reeves

Soul Garden Publications
Madbury, NH

Soul Garden Publications
Madbury, NH

Library of Congress Control Number: 2026906225
Paperback ISBN: 979-8-9947712-0-4
eBook ISBN: 979-8-9947712-1-1

Book cover and interior design by Christina Thiele
Editorial production by KN Literary Arts

Contents

Author's Note

Awaken every given day to divine light and listen to the messages within.

Beyond the physicality of ourselves we search for a place of peace—a place of rest and reflection that illuminates the meaning of our life, a sacred place that allows us to be and see our true selves without judgment, as spiritual beings in human form.

It is not in our minds.

The Soul Garden lies within our heart and higher self, one with Spirit.

It is a space wherein we are whole, accepted, loved, and supported at all times and in all we do. Unique to each of us, the garden is a sanctum, a place of limitless thought and freedom, opportunity and peace—a perfect blending and balance of all there is, all that has been, and all that will be.

Your Soul Garden, the sanctuary of your soul, has existed throughout time not to be created but to be found—a mystery not to unravel but to unveil.

Come walk with me on the golden pathway from your heart to the spiritual Soul Garden of serenity, understanding, and oneness with all there is.

May your journey be blessed with discovery and truth.

Sally Gallot-Reeves
Spiritual Gardener

Introduction

"The kiss of the sun for pardon,
The song of the birds for mirth,
One is nearer God's heart in a garden
Than anywhere else on earth."

—Dorothy Frances Gurney, "God's Garden"

These lines of poetry have had a special place in my heart for many decades—decades of gardening and building sanctuary spaces and decades of reflection and progressive enlightenment. My gardens (and all gardens) are my places of tranquility, places to commune with nature and my higher power. When I am in a garden, I am closer to God. There, I am my honest self.

Years ago, I began to visualize garden space beyond its physicality and saw pathways connecting me throughout my life and to my higher self. I reflected on the plants I had cultivated for different reasons and at different times: gardens to celebrate the births of my sons; plants given to me as friends celebrated my birthday or moved away; scraggly plants from the PTA spring fundraiser that looked at me like puppies waiting for adoption. They were all waiting to be loved into their full existence. I lovingly planted and nurtured them.

In time, I realized I created gardens to pray in. I created holy gardens with plants that reminded me of loved ones who had transitioned but remained pivotal influences in my life. My gardens and plants mirrored my emotions, desires, and beliefs in perpetuating life. They had a purpose beyond the beauty of the landscape, and I embodied their meaning when I knelt on the soil connecting with Mother Earth, Gaia. Thoughts flowed to me and then flew to paper, becoming the beginning of *The Soul Garden Within*. As an author,

I recognized this work was more than myself, and I knew I was continually guided to explore, discover, and reflect on it to eventually share with others.

While I was writing components of the book that I saw in the garden, I started sharing Blessings for the Day through my website, email, and social media. I felt divinely inspired and identified myself as a "spiritual gardener." As I have grown and matured, my belief is that writing and sharing *The Soul Garden Within* is my soul purpose. My higher calling is to share, encourage, and create opportunities for enlightenment for myself and others. We should all aspire to be spiritual gardeners.

The Soul Garden Within is a bridge connecting the physical self to the spiritual self. It is a book of progressive understanding, healing, and transformation. Each reader begins with their perception of their present reality and expands in their knowledge and awareness of their unique journey along life's pathways. We are all on the same journey to understand ourselves within the spectrum of infinite possibilities and experiences that life blesses us with.

Inside each of us is a Soul Garden, a sacred place of peace and serenity. It is the sanctuary we have created throughout our lifetimes with our thoughts, words, and actions. In the center of the garden is our Tree of Life, representing the interconnectedness and interdependence of our physical, mindful, emotional, and spiritual energies and resources—the communicators of self to higher self and Spirit. The Soul Garden is meant to be discovered and explored to its fullest extent so that we may continue to become what we choose to be.

The blessings of divine light, love, and spiritual grace allow us to make choices as we are intended to do as spiritual beings in human form. Choice is one of the highest gifts bestowed upon us as we emerge into the earthly realm. *The Soul Garden Within* helps us understand our choices, their outcomes, and their effects on our lives. It overlays the wisdom of universal and spiritual laws and principles and creates an opportunity for us to see that our experiences are guided by them all. By understanding the constants in life, we grow to understand where we are, where we have been, and where we want to be. Previous choices give us reflection and insight into future decisions and actions.

The Soul Garden Within is for everyone who searches for answers to everyday questions: Where am I? How did I get here? Where do I want to be? It is for those who seek a place wherein they are whole, accepted, loved, and always supported in all they do. It is designed for those who are newly awakened on their spiritual journey and those who are looking to expand further.

Chapters proceed in an orderly fashion, each one building upon the previous in content and depth. It is important to allow sufficient time to consider your relationship to the contents and answer the Discovery Thoughts questions in each chapter. In that way, dedicating space in your life to read, respond, and appreciate the awareness you gain maximizes your experience.

There are many successful ways to read and process *The Soul Garden Within* based on your personal preferences. You may choose to read individually, respond on your own, and plan to reread later, perhaps even discussing with others at another time. Or you may choose a group setting in a workshop or a book club led by a facilitator. *The Soul Garden Within* is designed to enhance the engagement of the reader as well as the facilitator role.

I believe there is value in sharing thoughts and responses and knowing how privileged you are to hear another person's life story. Through their experiences we become more aware of the limitless pathways in all gardens: what has been planted, what has been sown, and what has been connected. One of my readers chose to read one chapter at a time and then meet every other week with her mother to share their beliefs and gain insight into decisions they both had made in their lives. The reader said it was a beautiful gift to each of them to know the whole other person beyond their role relationship.

What is the soul? The soul as a concept has been in existence since the beginning of time. The word "soul" was recorded as early as the Egyptian hieroglyphics and in the writings of Socrates, Plato, and Aristotle. Over time, the definitions and meanings of the word have varied somewhat as they were influenced by cultures and religions. Prominent religions such as Christianity, Buddhism, Hinduism, and Islam all recognize the soul as the center of the physical self, the core, and the link to a higher power and life ever after. Spiritually, the soul is infinite and universal. It gives rise to our physical form as we emerge into the earthly plane and transitions with us at the time of our physical death. The soul is immortal.

In modern times, artists and authors depict the soul as a holy part of our body, frequently pictured with an eternal flame burning inside. People believe the soul resides within the heart and that it connects to a divine or universal power. The soul is the energy of your multidimensional being from inception to immortality. It embodies the true essence of yourself throughout your current lifetime and all your lifetimes. It influences your personality, identity, beliefs, and memory. The soul is the opening to spiritual connection, beyond the self to the higher self.

What is a Soul Garden? A garden is a living space that evokes images of beauty, peace, and tranquility. It displays the attributes associated with the seasons of our lives: the rests of winter, the germinations of spring, the bounties of summer, and the harvests of fall. A garden symbolizes the stages and years of our life events and experiences. It is unique to each of us and sacred.

You create your Soul Garden from the seeds of your thoughts, words, and actions. You grow it further with your experiences and choices. As you grow you can participate in and comprehend a wider spectrum of opportunities. Your Soul Garden will be familiar to you as you walk along the pathways guided by content and Discovery

Thoughts. You are safe and secure within the circumference of your Tree of Life, the tree wherein mind, body, and spirit grow together in energetic symmetry.

The paths we walk give insight into our life purpose—the reason we are blessed to live this life we are given. Each path leads us forward, with each step we take relevant and connecting to the next. There are no missteps. We learn from every passage, every choice, every day. We are here to learn in this lifetime and carry our wisdom forward. As we walk forward, we can assess our present circumstances and identify areas we would like to explore further. Through this exploration we can determine other choices. Choices and changes are a catalyst to our growth and the ability to identify our true, authentic selves.

There are several things that will help you align with the contents of this book and the flow of information from it. Know that you are guided on your journey. Each experience is a discovery and realization. As you grow, you change. As you change, you are enhanced.

First, remember to consciously breathe. Inhale a slow deep breath, pause, and exhale any extraneous thoughts and distractions. Breathe in the goodness and essence of the Soul Garden within. Repeat several times, visualizing the positive energy flowing to you and the scents of the earth and flowers. Continue to breathe until any distracting thoughts have evaporated and you can focus on your Soul Garden.

Scan some pages and quotes. Consider what you would like to receive by engaging with the contents and gaining knowledge and understanding of your life, your purpose, and your Soul Garden. Open your mind to words that whisper to you, and be aware that you are being guided by your higher self. Write these words down. Their meaning will become apparent at other times as you process the subject matter.

For the next step, create a personal motivational statement. This is a statement that reflects your inspiration and incentive to be one with your Soul Garden and to explore the paths before you. You can use this statement as a mantra before your reading and writing exercises to prepare your mind and emotions to connect with Spirit within this sacred environment. Start by thinking of things that you value and want to cultivate. Remember, you are becoming a spiritual gardener yourself! Then add a motivational statement. Motivational statements usually begin by referencing yourself, such as, "I am, I ask, I receive, I allow...." followed by words that describe what you desire to happen. You are creating an environment with your words that fosters your growth and alignment with goals. Your motivational statement opens your mind and establishes a channel to connect with your higher self.

Here are some examples of motivational statements:

* "I am blessed to be present in a place of surrounding love."
* "I am open to receive the goodness of truth that flows into my awareness."
* "I grow in thanks and gratitude when I am one with divine light and love."

My personal motivational statement is, "I ask to be blessed and guided to bring greater light and love into the world."

The scope and depth of information in this book is extensive. The contents give definition to physical and spiritual concepts and open you to a broader field of understanding. Your translation of the information sets your journey in motion. You need time to read, reflect, and journal. It is best to have a notebook or notepad nearby to write down your thoughts as you read.

As you begin each section, pause and center yourself. If you are in a group with a facilitator, they may choose to add guided meditation. Place your feet on the ground or floor and visualize yourself connecting with Mother Earth. Open your mind and emotions to the flow of ideas. Feel divine energy entering through your body's crown chakra, flowing down through your neck to your chest, and filling your heart space. Bring your motivational statement to the forefront of your mind and allow it to rest there. When you feel relaxed and open you are ready to proceed.

The Soul Garden Within is a book of progressive consciousness and enlightenment. It gives order to understanding the physical world and the concepts that lead to better understanding of the spiritual world and yourself. From self you connect to dimensions of the spiritual world and its relationship to all there is. Everything is connected. Everything is affected by the actions of other things, which create additional energetic movement. Everything is part of a bigger process and is in motion at all times. Know you are a world within a world.

The contents of *The Soul Garden Within* are divinely inspired. Chapters contain seed thoughts, quotes, universal and spiritual concepts, Discovery Thoughts, and affirmations. These elements promote your thinking and generate further ideas. Where do these thoughts come from? Each of us creates our own reality based on our mindfulness, ego, emotions, experiences, and responses. Thoughts arise *within the self*, *from the self*, and *beyond the self*. Examples of these include instincts, behaviors, and intuition. We are programmed to receive and communicate at all times.

Discovery Thoughts in each chapter help you assimilate and process what you have read and how it relates to yourself—your own life circumstances and experiences. You may want to document your reflections and ideas as well as your answers to the exercises. Discovery Thought questions give inspiration for you to consider your individual realizations, feelings, and insights from each section of the book. They are an opportunity to digest what you have read, perhaps discussed, and deciphered. They offer a chance to synthesize what you believe about yourself and your life at this moment in time.

If you are unable to respond to a Discovery Thought, please go back and reread the section preceding it when you are ready to restart. Determine a few words instead to describe what you feel. This could be as simple as, "I can't think," "I am too tired," or "I don't have time to consider this." When you begin again from a different framework, this acts as a placeholder. Those few words will step aside and allow new thoughts to surface. Life is a process of growth and regrowth. There are times when pauses in our activities allow for the subconscious mind to formulate deeper meaning and discernment of information that we are being asked to be aware of.

Following many of the Discovery Thoughts there is an affirmative statement. Affirmations are conscious, positive statements that promote and enhance our well-being. They set an intention, influencing the thoughts of the subconscious and conscious mind. They are similar to motivational statements in their positive message. Affirmations align the physical being (body/mind) with higher self (spirit) and project positive energy out into the universe for us and others to act upon. For these statements, complete part of the affirmation to continue the supportive thought that has been started. Affirmations bless and seal each section.

To begin, think of a positive statement that reflects a belief about yourself. This can be something existing or something desired. Affirmations often begin with "I am," "I do," or "I believe." Add to this a result statement that gives direction or definition to what you believe about yourself. Some examples:

* "I am blessed by angels every day. I embody their goodness."
* "I embrace the love that surrounds me. My love grows when I share it."
* "I trust in my ability to make choices. My choices are for my highest good."

Choose your environment. It is best to be in a place of calm where you can relax apart from the disturbances of everyday life. This includes phones, distracting noises, and miscellaneous people. Within this place of quietness be aware that every thought is a prayer. Light a candle or incense or play soft music in the background if you wish. Every thought is a vibration of energy from you flowing into the universe. Ask for this place and time to be blessed.

Quotes within the chapters add another dimension of thought and creative imagery. Many quotes are from notable people, artists, and healers. I believe they are autobiographical. I believe the person is conveying a pivotal thought in their lives that expanded their thinking. Their quotes allow us the privilege to see new life meanings by reading their words.

While you are reading you may hear thoughts coming to you. These are messages. I encourage you to record them to explore further. Whether you understand them or not, believe they are relevant to your journey.

There is extreme value in reviewing what you have written later (even years later), especially after significant life events occur. For example, I recently went back to chapter 2 searching for a greater understanding of my unexpected health circumstances and found that it answered my questions and fears. Time creates openings for growth and change, and what you write reflects a moment in a phase of your life. If you write with consciousness, your words reflect your reality to the best of your ability. Added knowledge and experience over time broadens your perspective and acceptance of the life you live and the life you choose to have.

I am honored and grateful that you, the reader, are choosing to walk with me through the Soul Garden. It is my heartfelt desire that your journey will expand your spiritual awareness and connection with all there is. Know you are blessed.

Dear Lord, may I see that I am becoming whole in your eyes.
May I see that I am part of the whole in mine.

Chapter 1

The Passageway

—Matthew Arnold, "Morality"

Relax into your physical being. Open your mind and consciously breathe. Allow your breaths to flow within you and through you, deep breaths of life into your heart.

The passageway opens, beckoning and enticing you forward to explore, to learn, to grow.

This is your journey of discovery and enlightenment.

Life Began in a Garden

What is the beginning of life—or the beginning of anything? Where does something begin and something end? Does it ever do either?

Everything is a process, and everything is within a process. Everything is connected and affected by what came before and after, what exists, and what is changing. On Earth, energy is transformed and manifested in tangible ways for us to begin to comprehend it. As we grow, experience, and expand we build progressive layers of consciousness. The beginning is therefore only a glimpse into what has been created and is creating. The *Soul Garden Within* does not start your journey; it continues it.

Life began in a garden as the story of Adam and Eve depicts. This could be the first story told or recorded to explain the beginning of human life on Earth. The story itself is not as important as the concepts it conveys about our humanness. In the Garden of Eden, we are given abundance in the place we are asked to live. Everything is before us and within our reach except that which is forbidden, what we are asked not to do. This is the beginning of intentional action, a choice that is contrary to instruction and the initial consequences of "right" and "wrong." It is the beginning of the polarization of needs, wants, desires, and our human weaknesses.

We are blessed with the gift of freedom and the ability to make choices: to make decisions that are for our highest good and the highest good of all or to make decisions only on our own behalf, the root of ego. With every choice there is action and then reaction. Results, outcomes, and consequences become a new reality we must evaluate. Adam and Eve both experienced the consequences of picking the apple. They rejected their abundant haven through their freedom of choice.

Abundance is a perception of wholeness in our lives, a feeling that everything we need and desire is available to us. We are free from worry and want. In the physical world, we associate abundance with security (love, money, housing, food), while in the spiritual world, we associate abundance with limitless creativity and our ability to manifest what we want. Abundance exists in all of us, always, and in multiple forms. It is readily available for us to access.

We are all creators. Our choices and actions activate energy moving outward that will initiate a response. These responses continue to move and impact other movements of energy that are beyond our sphere of consciousness. Because of this connectedness of energy from one (person or thing) to another ad infinitum, all become part of the energy process. We should remember then that what we choose and therefore activate has a life beyond ourselves. What is created within one is ultimately capable of connecting in time to all others.

"Creation is only the projection into form of that which already exists."

—Srimad Bhagavatam

Our Soul Garden is the creation of ourselves, our higher selves, and Spirit. It is a place where our choices can create abundance. In the garden we are always whole, always able to bring into being the life we are designed to have that serves our purpose. Our Soul Garden is vibrantly alive with living energy along the paths we walk—past, present, and future.

As we progress into Discovery Thoughts, think about what you are grateful and thankful for and what you would like to create in your life.

Discovery Thoughts

Take a moment and reflect on the abundance in your life. What things represent security? What things represent limitless creativity? What are you grateful for? Why?

....

Affirmation: "I am a dynamic source of limitless abundance. I create what I desire."

....

Now add an affirmative thought to continue your flow of positive energy: "I ..."

....

Consider your role on Earth as *Homo luminous*, a human being of light. We are designed in divine likeness and then we develop components and characteristics that make us unique individuals. Your soul is seeded in a physical vessel that expands in three dimensions: mind, body, and spirit.

"Since you are like no other being ever created since the beginning of time, you are incomparable."

—Brenda Ueland

You are capable of receiving and creating vibrational energy to manifest thoughts into a tangible reality. You are a life-giving form of the universe blessed with guidance and intuitive wisdom and responsible for your acts. This awareness brings immense opportunity and gifts into your life for you to utilize as you desire.

Think about your Soul Garden, a beautiful place of expanding life. When we tend our Soul Garden, abundance blooms from every plant and tree. Tended with gratitude and love, what we think, feel, and say is recreated in a living form following the universal law of cause and effect. New life flourishes from our actions.

Know that you are blessed to create on Earth the garden that is mirrored in your soul. You are empowered by divine light and love.

Discovery Thoughts

Picture your Soul Garden, your place of love and serenity. What do you see? Breathe in the aroma of blossoms. What do you feel?

....

Affirmation: "I am the beauty of my soul. I bloom with generosity, kindness, and love."

....

Now add an affirmative thought to continue your flow of positive energy: "I ..."

....

"The life we want is not merely the one we have chosen and made. It is the one we must be choosing and making."

—Wendell Berry

As you read this, you are using the skills of your mind, the bountiful gifts of cognitive development, thinking, and interpretation.

The human mind believes that by using logic we can understand the underlying purpose of life, but it is by loving acceptance of all experiences that our journeys gain trajectory. Credence opens us to the flow of universal energy and direction while our life purpose is an ever-evolving process of discovery.

Many of us search for meaning beyond our everyday lives—the source of things we cannot explain and the unexpected occurrences in our life. Life forces innately draw us to our place of origin, the ethereal plane. Behind the veil (the space between the physical and ethereal) the universe seeks to connect us to where we are from, assist us in determining where we are, and help us choose how to move forward.

As you physically emerge at the time of birth, you continue a subconscious energy connection to the ethereal life behind the veil. There are people who have memories of this connection, including life-purpose choices, while becoming the life-giving form they are meant to be. If you have insight into your ethereal life, hold it in the highest regard. Let your sacred connection come forward and give clarity and meaning to the choices you are making.

Our sacred soul is eternal, transcending time and choosing to live temporarily in a physical vessel to bring divine purpose, light, and love into the world. On Earth we are blessed by grace, benevolence, and faith that nurture and liberate us. We embrace peace, harmony, and balance to thrive within challenging and harsh environments and circumstances. By our thoughts, words, and actions we continue to create our Soul Garden.

You are your Soul Garden. You are the energetic manifestation of your gifts and the spiritual light you bring into the world. What you desire is the discovery of yourself. Journey inward.

The Tree of Life (Roots, Trunk, and Branches)

"Only when inspired to go beyond consciousness by some extraordinary insight does beauty manifest unexpectedly."

—Arthur Erickson

You are able to enter your Soul Garden through your heart. Place your hands, left over right, in the center of your chest and begin to take slow deep breaths, in and out, as you begin to visualize this sacred place. It breathes with you. It is filled with beauty and light so limitless it is beyond your sight.

In your Soul Garden, growth occurs in all directions in living, vibrating energy. As you walk forward you are bathed in a golden yellow light that guides you. In the center stands a majestic tree, your Tree of Life, rooted deeply into the vastness of the earth and reaching upward to the heavenly realms. Your Tree of Life is a symbol of your lives on Earth expressed in the fundamental principles of nature and the connective relationships between mind, body, and spirit.

People have written about the Tree of Life for centuries. To the Ancient Egyptians, the Tree of Life represented the hierarchical chain of events that brought everything into existence. The core rings, or spheres, demonstrated the order, process, and method of creation.

In Buddhism, the Tree of Life is known as the Bodhi tree, the tree of enlightenment, under which Buddha received his gifts of knowledge and understanding. In the book of Genesis in the Bible, the Tree of Life (which grew alongside the Tree of Knowledge) grew within the Garden of Eden and was considered the source of eternal life.

The Tree of Life also embodies karma, the sum of a person's actions in this and previous states of existence that is transferred by their soul through all lifetimes. As a result, the past karma that we embody influences us. In the present lifetime we are also creating new karma by continuing to make choices and respond to experiences. Being present, aware, and conscious of our actions is key to owning the responsibility of who we are and who we want to be.

"To put it in a modern way, karma can be explained as the tendencies of the soul, because karma is the imprint of memories from past lives that remain in each soul."

—Ryuho Okawa, *The Essence of Buddha: The Path to Enlightenment*

Consider the magnitude of karma as an energy force. Consider its role and purpose in our Tree of Life. Karma brings opportunity for awareness and insight into our lives. The gift of karma allows us to reexamine and make changes in our life that create new choices and direction.

Discovery Thoughts

As you continue to make choices in your life, how do past experiences influence you?

....

Physical, psychological, economic, and environmental factors create our outer world. How do you feel they impact your ability to live life fully?

....

Affirmation: "My life is blessed with karmic insight. I make decisions for my highest good as I live in the present."

....

Now add an affirmative thought to continue your flow of positive energy: "I . . ."

....

Consider the Tree of Life. It is you, in all your magnificent aspects. Trees have heritage, a lifeline, and ancestry. They are reflective of past and present and give promise to what can be created in the future. They are alive! At the center of your Soul Garden, your Tree of Life grows in divine light as the focal point of all your existence. The Tree of Life allows us to be a conduit from heaven to earth, from spirit to form.

Roots

"All theory, dear friend, is gray, but the golden tree of actual life springs ever green."

—Johann Wolfgang von Goethe

Your Tree of Life flourishes at the center of your Soul Garden, holding a command position to oversee and influence your growth. The roots of the Tree of Life represent your body, the physical vessel, anchored in the earth. In the spiritual world everything is mirrored. Roots lie in two planes, connecting beneath the soil and above the soil, providing connections to your past and present, to earth and spirit. As above, so below. And with this bilevel symmetry we can grow again in multiple dimensions. The heaven we desire on Earth is within us.

Beginning with the emergence of your ethereal seed, germination begins and heralds the process of coming into existence, growth, and development. Roots are strong, supportive, and grounding. They imply history and heritage, and they transport life-giving water and nutrients to sustain us. They balance all that grows above them and allow us to ground energy back into the earth, to Mother Earth, to nourish and bless it. From roots come new life and the connection to past life. The self is reborn each year with the seasonal enlargement of tree roots that bring fresh opportunity into the garden and our lives.

Discovery Thoughts

What are the expectations you have of your roots? Think of your family heritage and ancestry. How have these influenced you? Do you believe their influence is consistent with your beliefs and behavior?

....

What are the stressors in your life that can produce too much strain on your roots and cause damage? Now take this one step further and relate it to your physical body. What are the stressors impacting your life?

....

What are your expectations for your growth and wellness? Are you focused on achieving that?

....

Trunk

"Thinkers, listen, tell me what you know of that is not inside the soul?"

—Kabir

The trunk of your Tree of Life represents your spirit. Spirit is the essence of life, and the trunk of the tree provides a channel for energy communication and connection between all our dimensions, between physical, mindful, and higher self. Breathing inward and outward with palpable vibration, the tree exchanges vital nutrients to enrich the environment and itself. Energetic channels are its lifeline. It is strong and resilient. It does not sway or waver, which promotes our ability to stand tall and authentically.

Discovery Thoughts

What do you feel is the meaning of "spirit"? What words come to mind?

....

The trunk transports messages to roots and branches and influences involuntary functions as it grows, ensuring that we strive to our maximal potential. Inside the core of the trunk is a vein. Like the vessels in our body, the vein is meant to transport nutrients and messages that sustain life. The internal core protects the vein, our heart connection and energetic communicator to physical, to mind, and to our higher self/spirit. Consider this a vital passageway.

The trunk documents your life story in rings with every event, every year. The rings are a manifestation of growth years and lifetimes. Like stages of growth and development that outwardly display abilities and growth progress, the rings of the trunk are internally coded in such a way that you can access them at any time in your past, present, or future. Rings are embedded with life history in your core.

Branches

"Choice confers freedom—the freedom to embrace the new because it speaks to your soul and you are listening."

—Sarah Ban Breathnach

We grow and grow and expand. The multiple branches of the Tree of Life represent your mind, the infinite connections to think, feel, and understand your life. Branches connect you to the world, the universe, and all of nature. As branches grow they bifurcate and reproduce leaf buds along the stem. Consider these the "feelers" that venture out into the world to absorb and translate information into a usable form. Branches seek our greatest good and opportunities.

Branches symbolize our actions on three levels:

1. The creation of thoughts, perceptions, and understandings.
2. The incorporation of knowledge, wisdom, and emotions.
3. The recording of choices we make, the growth we incur, and the impact we have on ourselves and others.

The workings of the mind are influenced by many factors. Our thinking may vary with the tools we use, emotions, and feedback messages we send to ourselves. Tools include such things as analytics, beliefs, and previous outcomes. Emotions and ego are very persuasive in leading us in a direction, both positive and negative. The ego influences our thoughts and how we value ourselves.

Discovery Thoughts

What things in your life influence your thinking?

....

We know the mind creates, incorporates, and evaluates. This builds layers of thought, memory, and conclusions we have yet to investigate. Fortunately, growth gives us the maturity to relook and revise our thoughts and feelings, and to see things differently. We can incorporate a broader understanding of love and forgiveness and see things from the perspective of another person's point of view. The mind is generous, and one of our challenges is to open the aspects of the mind that allow for expansion in our thinking.

Our branches are functional in every season, providing new growth in the spring, shade in the heat of summer, harvest of the fruits in fall, and openings for light to pass in the dark days of winter. Through branching, we gain earthly and spiritual clarity that provides a platform from which to grow again.

The Tree of Life encompasses mind, body, and spirit. Roots represent the body, anchored in the earth and connecting upward to the trunk, your spirit self. Communicating below and above, the spirit trunk is your core balance in life and assists your branches in determining choices and experiences. The energy you absorb, transmit, and release is reflected in your growth.

The Tree of Life is a miracle of creation from inception, just as you are. Consider how expertly and meaningfully connected all components are designed and function. Looking at its majesty, we experience thankfulness and gratitude for our life, for all lives, for all that has been, is present, and will be. We know we are divinely inspired, and the purpose and intention of our lives is far greater than we can comprehend.

"Gratitude unlocks the fullness of life. It turns what we have into enough, and more. It turns denial into acceptance, chaos into order, confusion into clarity. . . . Gratitude makes sense of our past, brings peace for today, and creates a vision for tomorrow."

—Melody Beattie

Discovery Thoughts

Visualize your Tree of Life. What physical qualities are contained within the roots? How do you nourish yourself and the earth?

....

The trunk of the tree is your spiritual communicator. How does spiritual energy connect with your physical being, body and mind?

....

Your branches represent your mind. Look at how they reach out into the world. What are you reaching for? What are you searching for?

....

Affirmation: "I am a sacred Tree of Life. My mind, body, and spirit grow in divine light."

....

Now add an affirmative thought to continue your flow of positive energy: "I . . ."

....

Chapter 2

The Laws of the Universe

I have been repeatedly shown, and I have understood for a long time, that there is greater meaning in every experience than I initially comprehended. I have lived knowing this with trepidation and with joy. And because of that innate greater meaning, even when it's not yet visible, divine order and divine timing bless us with significant insight into the events in our lives. Hand in hand, one with our higher self, we are guided forward as the spiritual and physical truths reveal their deeper message and the path before us.

What is the difference between universal and spiritual laws? Universal laws are fundamental principles that govern all our earthly existence, our physical life. Universal laws are how energy, thoughts, and actions interact to create the world surrounding us and that which we encounter. Spiritual laws guide human behavior to achieve harmony within ourselves and the cosmos. They provide a moral compass for us to follow to grow and expand.

What is the meaning of a law or principle in the universal and spiritual worlds? Much of our learned behavior in life is based on established earthly rules and punitive laws. These can come from a place of authority, like government or religious doctrine, or expectations of family, teachers, social groups, and career. In science and math, a principle is a proven theory, whereas in society, a law is a command or mandate. They both exist prior to our actions to limit choices and behavior.

The principles and laws of the universe and the spiritual world are meant to give foundational structure to the world we live in. Within this structure our physical and mindful energy comes into alignment with soul energy, the connection with higher self and Spirit. This connection is our place of truth and authenticity.

What does truth mean to you? It may give you a feeling of security based on trust. It may build confidence that you are who you are meant to be, that you are where you belong. You journal, meditate, and pray, sharing your most personal and heartfelt thoughts. You ask for continued guidance. In trust, you believe that prayers are answered and that something will always come forward, even though there is no associated timeline for that occurrence. The universe is always working in your favor.

The laws of the universe and spiritual laws are constant in all situations and at all times. Their actions are not necessarily predictable, but they are repeatable. Given the same factors in the same type of situation, laws will adhere to the same principles. These guiding principles, repeating and perpetual patterns, are visible in all aspects of life. Many of these principles are cyclical: the hours in a day, the phases of the moon, the cycles of seasons, and the growth of the human body. These principles and laws exist at all times in all eternity.

The purpose of all laws is to guide and influence us in our choices and create outcomes that propel us forward. As you read this section you will find that the concepts of universal laws and spiritual laws are familiar to you. How they interrelate and rely on each other reveals a new depth of connectivity. Become aware of the meaning of the concepts and respect their impact. Universal and spiritual laws exist in parallel planes. Each accompanies us by moving along our situational timeline and sending intersecting energy as relevant events occur in both planes.

Understand that life experiences are steppingstones on your path of enlightenment. Experiences happen for your growth and expansion based on the choices you make. They give results for us to learn from. Our perceptions influence how we feel about situations, events, and people. We may view them as wanted or not wanted, positive or negative. Observe and notice what surrounds you. Use all your senses to evaluate the results of your choices and stay present in the moment. Avoid preplanning your responses to questions and events (if this, then that), but allow your feelings and responses to flow from the energy that arises from the mind and heart.

For example, there was a time in my early nursing career as a department manager that I felt that I had to be prepared for every situation that could arise and every question I might be asked. At the time I thought that meant I was very knowledgeable and totally in charge of my units, but I learned along the way that it was a very overt attempt to control circumstances and even the future— to control *everything*. What I also learned was that by preplanning my responses, I made assumptions about what might happen. I missed the opportunities to really listen to people and their needs. Experiences influence direction and next steps.

Divine Order, Divine Timing

"To everything there is a season,
A time for every purpose under heaven."

—Ecclesiastes 3:1 (NKJV)

The principle of connectedness is best seen in the relationship of divine order with divine timing. Things must exist in divine order before divine timing actionizes processes to move forward. When divine order is consistent on the physical plane it creates equilibrium in the spiritual world. Equilibrium is a derivative of the word "equal," meaning balanced. With balance, divine timing can align with spiritual energy to create movement, to create change.

What is divine order? Divine order intrinsically seeks to arrange things in a sequence, a series of events in a meaningful, prioritized relationship. This order sorts things, knowing what must come first before other things can proceed or exist.

Divine timing is more subtle. You may look back at situations and feel that you were just in the right place at the right time for things to happen. It is important to remember that you are given what you need when you need it. Divine timing goes beyond the material sense of needs and creates events for your well-being. Divine timing is omnipresent and ignites what is in your best interest and expansion.

Recently, I reviewed what I previously wrote regarding divine order and divine timing. I was searching for a greater understanding of my own health circumstances and my life journey. Unexpectedly, in October of 2018, I experienced severe lower back pain with left leg paralysis. Almost out of the blue, my whole life was changing. My health was uncertain, and my life predominantly became a healing journey.

Radiology testing revealed a large cyst that had grown through my lumbar vertebrae and was impinging on my spinal canal and spinal nerves. It had to be removed. Winter was approaching, and the flu was rampant. The earliest surgical date I could schedule was in December, more than two months away. Preoperatively, my life was dramatic. I was mostly confined to a wheelchair in the day and a recliner at night. I could not lie flat. I could go to the bathroom by myself, for which I am forever grateful. The days were endless and the nights hollow. My prayers reverberated in the darkness.

Our dog, Angus, is a terrier mix that we rescued from a gas station as a puppy. He looks like a baby Wookiee from *Star Wars* with fluffy beige fur all over. Angus is very perceptive and protective, and he hovered over me, sitting on an ottoman beside my recliner. Several nights after I began sleeping in the recliner, I felt Angus gently climb over me and lie vertically against my body. His head rested on my chest. When he lay atop of me, I couldn't move, and when I couldn't move, I had no pain. He stayed there every night and into the spring when I could again sleep in a bed. Blessed are the angels among us.

I was excited to finally move forward with surgery that December. I worked as a nurse in the hospital, and I knew many of the people taking care of me. I felt confident and assured. After surgery, my post-op course was painful and challenging, but I rejoiced each day at the renewal of feeling in my leg. I wore a large, hard back brace to keep my spinal vertebrae aligned. I had to regain strength and balance and learn to walk again. The priorities of the divine order were clear.

After five months of physical therapy, and despite some progress, I lost patience with the uncertainty of the length of time associated with my healing. My expectations had not been met, which led to dismay and feelings of depression. I turned to my book, *The Soul Garden Pathway: Discovery Guide*, for direction. I was relieved and reassured when I reread chapter 2. It did not promise anything, but it helped me understand divine order and divine timing from a higher perspective that I had not been previously aware of.

The pathway of my healing was not under my control. I was only to navigate the steps before me, trusting in the guidance and instructions I was receiving. I could not manipulate divine order nor ignite divine timing. Expectations are mischievous thoughts, and I think they are created by fear and the desire to control uncertain situations. My questions and fears were answered in chapter 2. The natural order of things gives rise to hope, and healing progresses in an orderly manner. All parts of the body, but especially nerves, require a great deal of time to heal. Time is a human measurement. Divine timing is the initiation of actions to move forward when things are aligned. I knew I could only physically do what I could do each day. The rest was not within my control. Knowing this truth fortified my trust and faith. Faith is not just a concept I believe in; it is and must be a daily practice.

It behooves us to be aware of these principles and their guidance as they assist us in being aligned with soul energy. The consistency laws and principles personify in the physical world and the equilibrium they symbolize in the spiritual world are reliable foundational references you can build upon. Know then that as you progress forward in your life, there are messages in the circumstances that surround you, and there are constants in all life circumstances. I grew to understand that divine order also included assessment of myself and my readiness to move forward. That is what I focused on as I healed. How could I align myself more closely with laws and principles to be one with these truths?

Divine order and divine timing rest on the principle of connectedness, the relationship of one entity to another. These concepts parallel the spiritual laws in their instruction and insight: to guide, to prepare, and to increase awareness. Each association has specific relational purposes we are meant to learn from. Our actions create bidirectional intentions. Energy projects outward into the universe and all those we interact with, while outcomes of that energy return to us. It is our heartfelt desire to be in a state of balance, and the universe guides us to maintain that balance and alignment with source energy, spiritual energy.

Living your life means walking a path of enlightenment. Walking forward, divine order and divine timing reveal information that guides you in the direction of service to your highest good and the highest good of all. Observing and listening are two key components to understanding these principles and your progress. In living your life, you may experience episodes of frustration and even anger when what you believe should happen does not, even when things appear to be ready and complete to actionize. Remember that we are living our earthly life for purposes beyond ourselves and to assist in creating changes that are optimal for us to live in with unity and love.

I have gained greater understanding and a new consciousness about being human. Yes, we are spiritual beings in human form, but we are also very human in every cell of our body. As such, we are subject to all conditions of being human: physical, emotional, psychological, and mindful conditions and all their associated vulnerabilities. My vessel responds to human conditions in the way it is intended with the abilities I am blessed with.

My life and wellness journey has continued with progressive spinal degeneration and four more surgeries, three in my lower back and the most recent in my cervical spine. Although I do not understand the *why* behind this pathway, I understand that I am not meant to. I believe I might use an explanation of *why* to try and control and even preplan my future. What I do know is that my mind, body, and spirit are always trying to realign with healing energy. My journey is a journey of faith and trust.

"The events in our lives happen in a sequence in time, but in their significance to ourselves they find their own order, a timetable not necessarily—perhaps not possibly—chronological. The time as we know it subjectively is often the chronology that stories and novels follow: it is the continuous thread of revelation."

—Eudora Welty, *One Writer's Beginnings*

In addition to divine order and divine timing, there are four other universal laws: dependency, sequencing, adjacency, and synchronicity.

Dependency is a relationship of power. To strive for independence, we must first experience dependency. When something is dependent, the more powerful factor must be present and recognized as powerful by the reliant factor. Through episodes of dependency, we can gain confidence and gradually become more independent selves. We are born into the world in our most dependent state, physically and mindfully. At the beginning of life, and sometimes at the end, we must totally rely on others to continue to survive. As I have experienced, this can also occur at times of serious illness or accident when our health and abilities are significantly compromised. Survival is a basic need and the most vulnerable state of being.

When we are aware that there is a relationship between dependency and power and that we are influenced by it, we are better able to see choices that promote our personal freedom. If we ignore relationship patterns of dependency and their influence on our choices, the outcomes we achieve may be less than what we desired and what we intended. Because we are influenced by those with power in a dependent relationship, our decisions may reflect more of their desires than our own.

Independence is an increasing aspect of our physical and psychological maturity and expanded authentic self. Gaining independence, and therefore our own power, is a process that spans many years. It involves physical and psychological development and maturation and the ability to understand ourselves, our needs, and our desires. Gaining independence brings forward opportunities, challenges, and choices. Circumstances of our lives, such as those that influence security and safety for instance, may influence how quickly we are forced to become more independent while compounding the difficulty in accomplishing that process.

When I matured in my ability to make decisions best for my own life, I also learned that my choices do not have to be permanent. I can revise them! When you are responsible for your choices, the ability to revise and make changes are within your purview and what is in your best interest.

At times, we may also establish a dependent relationship with substances or behaviors. Initially these may be motivated by what we think we will gain, but they culminate in experiencing what we may lose. When we grow and gain confidence, we become aware of choices that are best for our personal well-being. We learn to trust our judgment.

I have come to know that struggle is being uncomfortable with the circumstances that surround you. To me, this discomfort is a motivating force. It creates opportunity to look beyond the obvious and harness the resources that are available to you. You are never alone or abandoned. Struggle often makes us more aware of our strengths and the gifts of self-reliance as we rise to meet objectives. Struggle is a key component in searching for our truth and purpose.

Sequencing is a relationship of order of a series of related units. When these are aligned, they become building blocks that we can understand and utilize. To proceed, to move forward, factors must adopt positions one after the other. A sequenced pattern is the opposite of random and may follow a hierarchical pattern, a vertical alignment. Things in a sequence may be part of a divine order, but they do not require divine timing to influence the order. They are choices in our past or present day that are useful in affirming who we want to be and how to move forward.

The progression of my nursing career followed a sequenced order that I could not see at the time. As I moved throughout the United States, I made some of my work choices consciously in relation to my goals while others I made coincidentally and subconsciously. I saw clearly later how a culmination of knowledge and skills had prepared me to move forward as an RN and as a director of multiple departments. Without that sequencing I do not think I would have been qualified to assume such a diverse role.

Things that occur in a sequenced or successive pattern make us aware of what has been available to us and how we have made choices. Sequenced events help us understand how we have progressed along our life path following the steppingstones laid out before us. They reveal choices that were to our benefit and those that did not yield a desired result. We learn from them so that in the future, by wisdom and grace, we will make choices that are optimum in living our life fully. I like to think of my nursing career as a key component of my path to enlightenment.

There are many complex sequencing patterns in our lives that exist to assist us in navigating paths and obstacles. Sequencing patterns repeat in similar situations to promote our understanding and to help us embody learnings into our consciousness. When we can see sequencing patterns for the positive or negative effect they have on our lives, we can make decisions and choices from a higher perspective of awareness.

I had a friend who lived across the street from me in New Jersey who also had young children. She and I both worked part-time, and we would trade babysitting hours to help each other out. Her children always had plenty of clothes and toys, and she was always showing me new things she had bought for herself and her home. I expected that she and her husband must be making a much higher income than we were—until the day a truck pulled up in front of her house and the repossession people took everything. Everything she had was either purchased on credit or rented. She was devasted, embarrassed, and speechless. She stayed at my house until her husband came home later that afternoon. I offered them dinner, but they said they were fine. That evening they left in his truck, and I never saw her again. Life has a way of repeating opportunities for us to learn from them and *until* we learn from them. I was clearly shown that what might appear to be real on the surface is not necessarily what is real. I also lost a friend, and I had another learning opportunity to remember to bless and let go of what is beyond my control.

Adjacency is a relationship of factors that influence your actions and outcomes. This relationship exists in a position relative to your present situation and may be temporary or permanent, obvious or intuitive. These elements convey information about a person, place, or thing relative to a moment in time and serve to guide you to promote your safety, health, and growth. In choosing a place to live, for instance, cost, location, school systems, access to services, size of home or property, and distance to work all influence your choice of residence. You may determine one factor is more important than the other, but they all align horizontally in their discovery. Adjacency factors may be subjective or objective. Based on their vibrational energy, what you feel about them, it is possible to assess the factors' negative and positive attributes and receive guidance about them. The role of intuition, your "gut feeling," is prominent as it sends vibrational energy absorbed from the environment and people involved to you. I have always found these intuitive messages and feelings to be correct in guiding me forward or back.

Synchronicity is a relationship of meaningful events without an evident connection. Synchronistic events occur in parallel planes that intersect in a moment of time. Because they are seemingly unrelated, people often misinterpret them as coincidence or accidental happenings, but their connection to your life is always meaningful. These presumed coincidences provide an association from one experience to the next that promotes thought and further action.

When we trust in the universal flow of energy, synchronicity is divine guidance in energetic form. Synchronistic events exist in our lives as instructional messages for us to act upon. Synchronicity realization requires mindful openness to consider factors beyond our understanding and respond intuitively following our inner guidance. An event can reveal to you that you are on the right path and making choices that are best for your life, so it is wise to spend meditative time considering their importance.

I began collecting inspirational articles, spiritual books, and meaningful quotes years ago, beginning in adolescence—just random pieces I was attracted to. I journaled my thoughts and stored completed notebooks in cardboard boxes. Decades later, I wrote and published a book of poetry called *Between Shifts*, which touched on my own experiences and insights into the human behavior and frailty I witnessed when I worked in nursing. My poetry book ignited my desire to write more, express more, and be more. My back surgery in 2018 presented me with an unwanted opportunity to do this because when you cannot walk or work, you can write. At first, I focused on daily journaling. It was therapeutic and served a purpose of spiritually connecting me to my higher source energy. I could not garden, which is my passion, but instead I visualized my spiritual garden, the Soul Garden. My family brought down my cardboard boxes from the attic and opened them for me. They were a long-hidden treasure.

As I reviewed my written materials and associated keepsakes, I found that they formed connections and were related. When I sorted them in an orderly way they created a beautiful and meaningful picture. More than that, everything fit together, and I had all the pieces I wanted to write something. I wrote and began to follow the path before me as I asked for divine guidance. My second back surgery in 2020 was similar to the first. There were compression fractures of my vertebrae above my previous surgical site. My left leg was paralyzed again, and I was in severe pain. I prayed and wrote more. As I result, I birthed and published *The Soul Garden Pathway: Discovery Guide* in 2021.

Synchronicity is a relationship of meaningful events without an evident connection, but when we trust in the universal flow of energy, synchronicity is divine guidance in energetic form.

I am so very grateful for the divine guidance I received and continue to receive.

Divine timing is a relationship of alignment with divine order. When the components of a process align, they create order and balance and can be activated. Like a catalyst, divine timing is the trigger that stimulates the progression of all things.

"Things come suitable to their time."

—Enid Bagnold

Divine order and divine timing principles give us perspective into the meaning of situations, relationships, and outcomes. When we observe from an elevated place of awareness and faith, we are guided to see their arrangement as a whole for the purpose of generating the best possible outcomes at a given time.

Discovery Thoughts 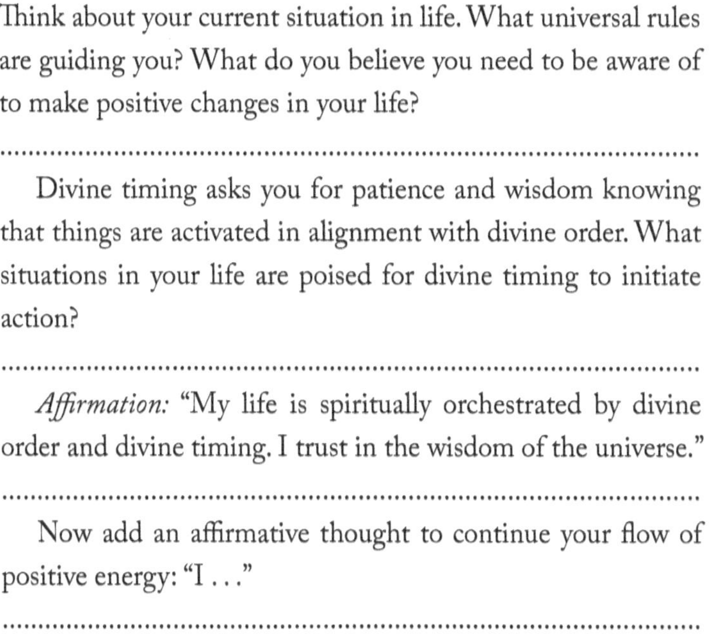

Think about your current situation in life. What universal rules are guiding you? What do you believe you need to be aware of to make positive changes in your life?

....

Divine timing asks you for patience and wisdom knowing that things are activated in alignment with divine order. What situations in your life are poised for divine timing to initiate action?

....

Affirmation: "My life is spiritually orchestrated by divine order and divine timing. I trust in the wisdom of the universe."

....

Now add an affirmative thought to continue your flow of positive energy: "I . . ."

....

Spiritual Laws

"As long as one keeps searching, the answers come."

—Joan Baez

Both universal laws and spiritual laws provide tools for our growth, expansion, and understanding, and both work with divine order and divine timing for our highest good and the highest good of all.

When you encounter resistance in your life—the irritating uncomfortable feeling that something isn't right—there are forces competing for your source energy. You can view any resistance you encounter as disharmony: a message that your situation and/or actions are not in keeping with spiritual guidance. This can happen when unwanted change occurs, and we try to block it from happening. Perhaps you are being assigned new responsibilities in a group but already feel overwhelmed. Resistance is a message that asks you for clarity. There is a push/pull feeling as the direction your mind or physical being is going fluctuates and you analyze positive aspects of the choices with the negative ones. This is a time to pause, reflect, and consider. Efforts to push through will not lead you to the lasting results you desire. Guidance always directs you in a positive way and asks you to pause, observe, and reflect. It asks you to be honest with yourself and others.

An important thing to remember is that resistance is a teacher. You are being given the opportunity to carefully consider your choices and way forward, and to determine if this is truly best for you. Resistance brings emotions to the surface and intuition to the forefront. It asks for honesty in contrast to pretense—pretending that everything is fine when, in fact, it is unbalanced and awry.

There are also times when you feel resistance persist despite your best efforts. Resistance is not a question of right or wrong but one of differences in perspective, process, and approach. Relationship disconnects bring about physical symptoms such as headaches, indigestion, and sleeplessness. In one occurrence with a supervisor, it occurred to me that the intensity of my beliefs was an obstacle. It seemed that in every situation that arose between us there was conflict, certainly disagreement, and unresolved issues. Separate from the individual, I had to determine if I could or could not change, and if I did change my thinking (and values) could I continue to live in my truth and authenticity? When there is confusion, I know I need to listen to my inner voice. Over time, I felt it was best to step back and pursue other positions. As soon as I made that decision, I felt relieved and other opportunities became available. It was not an emotional decision; it was a guided decision.

Sometimes we can make small changes or compromises and resolve the dynamics that create resistance. If you experience resistance, ask yourself if you need to improve communication or modify your commitments and goals. In the last phase of my nursing career, I became the hospital's healthcare project director overseeing all major capital budget projects. These included electronic medical record installations, process and workflow redesigns, and construction. In addition to the responsibilities staff already had to their units, we were asking them to attend multiple meetings and work on associated planning. Early on it was evident that schedules and workloads were too demanding and opposition surfaced. While the other administrators involved and I took these concerns very seriously, we had to balance those needs with project timelines and cost—hence my resistance. After careful consideration, we initiated multiple strategies to address the issues, including developing subcommittees, recording Zoom meetings instead of requiring in-person time commitments, developing an internal project portal, and restructuring my schedule to meet with individual leaders to proactively understand needs and workflow. These changes allowed for some effective breathing room and a more realistic approach to utilizing resources. If not for those initial feelings of dismay and frustration, we never would have found that better and ultimately more successful way to move forward.

> *"And those who were seen dancing were thought to be insane*
> *by those who could not hear the music."*

—Anonymous

As you explore your Soul Garden, the following spiritual laws are relevant to your understanding and growth. Used as a metaphor, growth appears in the Soul Garden with the planting of seeds, sprouting of shoots and stems, and creation of blossoms. There are six spiritual laws visible in the Soul Garden: the law of divine oneness; the law of attraction; the law of inspired action; the law of cause and effect; the law of compensation; and the law of polarity.

The law of divine oneness promises that everything is interconnected and therefore interrelated. Connection projects outward from you through energy vibrations. All our actions create energy we propel out into the universe. This vibrational energy attaches to other energy and stimulates further movement. Every word, thought, belief, desire, decision, and action will have an impact on you and the world. You may not immediately see or feel the results, but they have been initiated and will become apparent in one form or another.

This can occur when you ask for specific donations to benefit a charity or family in need. One person's kindness becomes magnified and others adopt it. An advertised donation goal prompts others to know what is still needed. Everyone feels the success of generosity in assisting others.

The opposite of divine oneness is fragmentation. When we resist or choose abruptly to go in another direction, we leave pieces of a process disconnected. They remain dormant until brought forward again by conscious thought and then activated.

The law of attraction tells us that like attracts like, that the energy that emits from our physical being—our mindfulness, emotions, words, and actions—acts as a magnet to attract energetic forces. You attract what you project physically, verbally, behaviorally, and vibrationally. This also applies to your thoughts and manifestations as you create what you focus on. Additionally, you attract what you are in the world. Simply put, you are attracted to what you are and what you give out. Love is the highest form of vibrational energy that we create.

The opposite of attraction is energy that is repelled, like a magnet when it will not connect with the opposing node. There are times when we encounter negative energy that makes us feel uncomfortable. We may even feel it as a personal affront. This is repelling energy. This is guidance that tells you to step back and reconsider its value and purpose to yourself. You are responsible for maintaining your integrity and balance. An important thing to remember is not to absorb another person's negative energy.

The law of inspired action instructs us that to live life fully we must actively pursue our goals. This includes thoughtfully visualizing what you desire and taking inspired, dedicated steps toward that vision. Each step, no matter how small, moves you in a direction closer to your purpose. You do not need to clarify purpose first. All movement allows you to reassess, realign, and change course as needed.

The opposite of inspired action is random action, which can be impulsive and not purposeful. We are asked by Spirit to mindfully pursue goals that promote our well-being and purpose on Earth. This requires consideration of where we are and where we wish to be, what we have done and what we wish to create. On Earth we are meant to bring more spiritual light and love into the world.

Discovery Thoughts

All steps are learnings and will therefore give you feedback and further direction. Where are your steps leading you? Do you feel a sense of fulfillment and contribution? Is your heart asking you to reconsider your present situation or continue on this journey?

The law of cause and effect explains that all actions have a corresponding reaction. Causality is an attraction where one event or object (the cause) contributes to the production of another, the effect of its energy. These results may be desired (positive) or undesired (negative). This law is reproduceable in science, math, physics, and by what we attract into our lives. Positive creates positive; negative creates negative. In the spiritual world, the corresponding reaction is an answer to prayer. We know that what we ask for in prayer is always answered in divine order and divine timing for our highest good and the highest good of all.

Trusting in this law allows us to trace the source of things. If we are open and honest with ourselves, we can assess how returning results have been initiated. You cannot exclude something from cause because you do not wish to think that it has the power to affect an outcome or that you have created an undesirable outcome. Outcomes may or may not be related to your intention, and it is important to retain an element of objectivity when analyzing results.

The law of compensation promises that you will receive what you give out. This is like the universal law of attraction. Compensation, or the return on your energy investment in your highest good, does not have a time frame. Sometimes the path you walk is a long path. There may be detours and roadblocks along the way. You should view your life purpose as a continuum of work and steps toward your goals with noticeable achievements along the way. Your purpose may become clearer as you walk the path before you. Think of it as a process. Life is a process. We need to remember that life events are situations happening *for* us, not *to* us.

Whatever we need will be provided. There is a distinction between need and want. As a rule, however, you will always receive what you give out and what you need. In considering what you need, the energy you put out will always return to you to fulfill a primary need, one that you can build upon. That need may not be fulfilled in the way you expected or imagined. Compensation comes in many forms, so you may not recognize it at first. Faith ensures that all situations occur in our highest good. If we move forward in trust, putting forth our best effort, Spirit rewards us with what we need for our growth and expansion.

The law of polarity tells us that everything has an opposite, and the very existence of these opposites allows us to better understand our life and the natural order of things. It teaches that dualities, like hot and cold or high and low, are two extremes of the same thing. If I am confused or wondering about the value of something, I often think of its opposite. I ask myself, "What if this weren't present?" This thinking leads me to expand my thoughts and ideas and see processes that come forward to assist me in multiple ways.

Our goal in living is to exist in the center balance, the core balance within us, in harmony with higher self and Spirit. Balance helps us to remain neutral and modify our reactions to daily events. It allows us to stabilize the forces that pull us in one direction or another, between the light and the dark, the positive and the negative, the truth and illusion. If we are in balance (think of a boat rocking on the waves), we can then be in alignment with Spirit (think of the mast of a boat reaching upward). This law emphasizes the interconnectedness of opposite forces, showing that they not only coexist but are also essential for balance and harmony in the universe and our lives.

> *"Each place along the way is somewhere you had to be*
> *in order to be here."*
>
> —Dr. Wayne Dyer

Spiritual laws constantly weave into our lives, affecting and intersecting all aspects. They are the threads by which we are guided to assess our choices in the fabric of our lives. They give us instruction in our behaviors and the ability to understand events and situations in an objective, mindful way. Every thought and action projects out into the world and initiates a response from others and the universe.

We are empowered by these laws to utilize them consciously and effectively to create abundance and bring love and light into the world.

Discovery Thoughts

Reflect on your life path, the path you walk. What spiritual laws are evident in the outcomes you have experienced? How have these created prosperity in your life?

....

Spiritual laws continuously guide us. Which laws do you consciously incorporate into your daily processes and practices?

....

Affirmation: "I embrace spiritual guidance. I ask for what I desire. I receive what I project into the universe."

....

Now add an affirmative thought to continue your flow of positive energy: "I . . ."

....

Chapter 3

The Human Experience

Birth: Our Emergence

Life on Earth brings forth opportunity. It is the life we choose and the life we search for in the same moment. In return, we are asked by Spirit to pursue our highest good for the highest good of all.

When you are born into the earthly world it signifies the end of the embryonic-fetal stage of development and maturation. Although we usually think of this in nine-month periods of time, time is not an absolute measurement in any life process. Birth is an experience within our lifetimes and a passageway from initial formation and growth that serves to prepare us to survive on Earth. Our soul and connection to Spirit accompany us in all phases of life and transitions.

See your life reflected in a deep pool of water that mirrors the heavens above you. Your face appears again and again within images of sky, and the sky within you, until all eternity projects into the pool—the last, minutest image, which is the seed, the life incarnate.

> *"The true joy of life is not in the grand gesture but in the consecration of the moment."*
>
> —Kent Nerburn

Human experience begins with creation and continuously evolves as a journey of awakening. In her book *Simple Abundance*, Sarah Ban Breathnach tells us this: "Remember, before anything exists on earth, it exists fully formed in spirit. The Great Creator does not play favorites; each of us came into being to carry on the re-creation of the world through our gifts."

The word "reincarnation" expresses the philosophical and spiritual concept of our soul's rebirth. In Hinduism and Buddhism, reincarnation was believed to be a passage of enlightenment, and both Socrates and Plato included this philosophy in their teachings.

Tribes of Indigenous North Americans, including the Zuni and Mojave, believed that reincarnation also includes the ability of the soul to emerge in other life forms such as animals and birds.

Spiritually, reincarnation represents our conscious choice to purposefully be of service on Earth to create good and bring forth enlightenment. Your soul is you and therefore reincarnates the true essence of who you are. We energetically configure our next lives behind the veil, which is the space between the ethereal and the physical, and proceed in faith without guarantee of outcomes. Each of our reincarnate births is of our choosing. They are rekindled opportunities to pursue life purpose and a life of service. With each lifetime we have the opportunity to experience illumination (ascending levels of understanding) and expansion associated with our soul's purpose. All life on Earth is a series of steps, processes that lead us forward on our path, but it is always our continued choices that create the directions we travel.

Let's ask Spirit to guide us in the following exercise. This can also be a facilitated meditation:

* Close your eyes and take a few slow, deep, cleansing breaths. Exhale softly and slowly. Center yourself.

* Continue taking slow, deep breaths as you connect with the energy surrounding you. The energy is a soft, warm cloud. You are safe here. You are safe to go back in your mind, way back to the time of life in the womb. It is soft, warm, safe. Do you see the beautiful child you are?

* Something is changing. You are being moved into a smaller space. Still safe, still warm. Labor has begun. Visualize yourself as a newborn now propelled from a warm fluid-filled sac through a tunnel and into a bright environment. It's colder. It's unfamiliar. It's bright light!

❋ "Where am I?" your beginning awareness asks as you cry out in a reflex response. You can hear sounds but do not know that the loud cry spontaneously arises from within you, your first outward communication to your new Earth life.

❋ Something moves you. You are held by strong hands and no longer floating or free to roam. Your eyes open, but your vision is not clear. You hear and feel but are unable to determine meaning. Soon you are placed with a mother and encouraged to nurse. Something new, the warmth of skin. Warmth. Your infantile sense of smell and taste begin to intake new stimuli and processes.

❋ "What is this? Where am I?" You, joy of creation, have arrived! This is the beginning of knowing your new life, of knowing who you are.

❋ Take a few minutes and review this visualized birth experience. Who is there? What do you feel?

Discovery Thoughts

What feelings came forth as you reenacted your birth? Do you feel secure? Is this a pleasant experience? Remembering that birth is your first earthly experience, is there a message you take away from this? Is there a message that you have kept with you all your life?

....

Affirmation: "I am a divine being of light and love. I am blessed by the grace of God."

....

Now add an affirmative thought to continue your flow of positive energy: "I . . ."

....

Life is a journey of awakening on a path of enlightenment as we pursue abilities, growth, and purpose. We experience illumination—sacred revelation that lights our way. It is through this illumination that we gain insight and understanding of where we are and where we are going.

Choice

We make choices both consciously and subconsciously. A conscious choice includes the mind's awareness of itself and its surroundings. Regardless of the outcome, these choices are intentional and purposeful.

A subconscious choice can be spontaneous, habitual, or reflexive. Without thinking, words and actions are automatic and repetitive. These can happen again within similar circumstances when you have adopted a response that you believe has some benefit for you.

To understand your choices and change those that do not promote desired results requires a conscious decision-making process. If you can identify and understand the situations, events, and actions that trigger undesired responses, you can reframe them within your mind. This requires diligence and a commitment to change.

The subconscious mind is an aspect of the physical self that stores memories and events as karma that can influence our thoughts and actions. Karma is the internal imprint of feelings, emotions, and perceptions. Within the subconscious these encounters build a library of interpretational references from which we draw upon in future time. Karma serves as an inner compass alerting us to situations and decisions that are important for our growth. In the evolution of our lifetimes, karma transfers with us upon reincarnation. We are gifted in life with recurring situations by which we can reconcile karmic remnants (the imbalance within) to live authentically in peace and harmony.

Often we talk about karma as being either good or bad, but

when karmic energy is stored, it has no such attachment. Our minds choose to translate karma, something that occurs on an energetic level, and label it so that it may be understood on a physical level. True understanding of karmic influence requires introspection and thoughtful consideration to allow the energy to speak for itself.

Karma within yourself is also stored in your Tree of Life. Like other experiences and knowledge, karmic energy leaves markers within the rings of the core of your tree. Remember that the trunk/core is your spiritual self and the communicator from roots (the physical) to branches (the mind). A real-life example of this is the occurrence of changes to width and dimension of tree rings in an actual tree during its lifetime. If the tree is cut down the rings are exposed, and scientists can identify years of drought, fire, and disease. Historically these rings are measured in years and are parallel to chronicled events. When we choose differently to promote better outcomes for ourselves, we release components of stored karmic energy.

Phases of Life
(The Ethereal, Physical/Spiritual, and Transitional)

Life as we know it is a continuum in three phases: the ethereal; the physical/spiritual; and the transitional. These phases repeat in the same order in all our lifetimes.

The Ethereal

We think of the ethereal as a heaven with all the human-associated images: the puffy white clouds with cherubim and seraphim, archangels with massive spreading wings, and harps of gold in a majestic place of peace with pearly gates and a god on a throne. Sound familiar? But what if the ethereal were another dimension of spiritual energy somewhere within the vapors of the universe? And within this ethos of existence, you were pure energy as well, the energy of your soul? What if your purpose in being this energy was to create all things imaginable: goodness, love, abundance, and peace? And every now and then, what if your soul energy chose to be recreated again in physical form? Would you not be bringing heaven to Earth?

"How we remember, and what we remember, and why we remember form the most personal map of our individuality."

—Christina Baldwin

In the ethereal, we choose life purpose, and our soul emerges past the veil to be physically alive on Earth. Most often we do not remember the ethereal plane. The veil closes in an amnesiac episode to allow us to be fully present as a human being, to engage in all aspects of human life with all life forms. We are given the opportunity to rediscover our authentic self as we evolve in human form and aspire to be one with Spirit.

Most world religions, sects, and doctrines identify a passage of life on Earth and a life thereafter. Consider your beliefs—all your beliefs—as valid. We are the products of our upbringing, experiences, and culture. What we do know is that in everyone's life there is a birth, a time of living, and an ending in the form of physical death. We also know that within these teachings there is some reference to a soul—a higher self or spirit within us. This leads us to know that there is something more powerful beyond ourselves.

These are age-old questions:

* Where do we come from?
* What lies behind the veil?
* How do I appear in the afterlife?

If you believe in reincarnation, you understand that there is time and space devoted to transition, re-creation, and the transmission of the soul. It exists beyond the realms of our understanding of the factors that perpetuate life. It exists beyond the dimensions of our mind. Without physical evidence but with the knowledge of energetic transmission and spiritual connection, we can conceptualize the ethereal as a place of pure spiritual energy, an energy that transcends all barriers.

In the ethereal we choose to reincarnate, and in so doing reassign our life direction.

I believe life direction, or purpose, is based on very broad categories with high perspective and little detail. The details are revealed as we live in physical form, in our life experiences and choices. A succinct way of summing it up is to say our ideal life purpose is to live our lives for our highest good and the highest good of all. The intent is not to simplify but to enlarge our scope of awareness. Know then that what you wish to create in your lifetimes is achievable through your choices and experiences.

The Physical/Spiritual

In this phase of our life, the world inside of us becomes a dynamic network of vibrational communication and interpretation, channeling thoughts and messages. Energy flows to us and through us, which we utilize to grow, experience, and further develop. We expand in many dimensions, always trying to create a world we wish to live in. Conscious thoughts become our reality. Our connection with Spirit is our lifeline.

* We develop, experience, and expand as a physical, mindful, spiritual being.
* Our life within the physical vessel is a complex connection between growth, communication, relationships, experiences, and mindfulness.

❋ Growth allows us to gain survival skills, abilities, strength, and mobility.

❋ Communication fosters knowledge and understanding of ourselves and the world we live in. We communicate needs, desires, emotions, and expectations.

❋ Relationships include those with ourselves; our family, community, and social sphere; and our environment.

❋ Experiences guide us, promote learning, and give us further choices.

❋ Mindfulness is awareness. In our lifetimes we continue to increase awareness of self, beliefs, knowledge, emotions, and that which is beyond our humanness.

Our bodies are holy vessels that house our souls so we may live on the earthly plane. The body requires nourishment, respect, healing, and activities that promote its optimal functioning. We are the stewards, the caretakers, responsible for its care. Dr. Wayne Dyer, in his book *You Are What You Think*, gives us this valuable insight: "You would never abuse something that you thought was valuable . . . well, the same thing is true of yourself. If you think of yourself as valuable, very important, very significant as a human being, then you would never, ever abuse yourself, and you wouldn't allow someone else to abuse you. Most abuse people endure . . . comes from a belief, a fundamental belief, that what I am abusing isn't worth anything."

Our body and mind are our connections with the physical world, while our spirit connects us to the ethereal/the universe. We go through our sacred heart to Spirit and to access our Soul Garden. In living our life, we create our reality through perceptions and choices. Our journey is based on the steps we take to move forward. Connection with Spirit provides masterful guidance.

We have many opportunities and choices before us. The desire to discover our truth and authenticity leads us closer to higher self and Spirit. We are gifted when we open ourselves to vibrational communication and interpretation of thoughts and messages coming toward us.

*"The opposite of life is not death. The opposite of death is birth.
Life has no opposite."*

—Eckhart Tolle

The Transitional

When the human body can no longer support our biological needs, it weakens and physically experiences death. We experience many types of transitions within our physical life that all lead to further growth. Death is the final transition in an episode of one human lifetime, while our soul ascends to incorporate again into the ethereal.

Transition is a passage of change and metamorphosis. Transitions bridge episodes of learnings with levels of maturity, allowing us to evolve again. In the physical form, transition represents a shift in mindfulness and beliefs. In transitioning, we have the opportunity to release that which no longer serves us: emotions, choices, regrets, sadness. The release of negative energy, which comprises a very heavy density and weight, promotes transition.

Transformation as part of the process of ascension on Earth does not necessarily require a physical death. We can see it in progressive steps in some people as they become more and more aligned with Spirit. In transitioning we become free to engage in new beginnings. We are able to create through re-creation of who we desire to be and who we are asked to be.

In the transformational phase of life after our physical death, we focus our time on aligning with and incorporating the energetic ethereal world. We ascend, rising higher. We are one with our soul in reviewing our earthly life. There is no quantitative way to measure this in time; changing from a physical form to an energetic form is a very complex process.

The three phases of life (the ethereal, the physical/spiritual, and the transitional) are continuing passageways for us to enter new dimensions of a spiritual being in human form. Possibilities are endless. We create our own reality and, therefore, the journey.

Discovery Thoughts

What are your earliest recollections of your childhood? What emotions do you associate with them?

....

As you live your life, give thanks and gratitude for your sacred vessel that houses your soul. How do you care for your body to promote its physical (body/mind) well-being?

....

Affirmation: "I am the incarnation of my highest self. I reflect my wholeness in all stages of growth."

....

Now add an affirmative thought to continue your flow of positive energy: "I . . ."

....

*"Everyone is a house with four rooms, a physical, a mental,
an emotional, and a spiritual."*

—Traditional Indian Proverb

Spiritual Life Within the Vessel

Integration is the process by which connecting parts are incorporated into a whole. These parts are equal in importance to achieve maximum benefit yet distinct in their own function and attributes. The body, mind, and spirit are three integrated forms of life energy within our physical being. In its truest form, everything is energy, everything is a process, everything is symmetrically balanced.

The body is a temple, a holy place that is made in the image of our creator. It is a miraculous work of art, structure, and function that nourishes our physical being and mind. The human body is a universe unto itself, wherein every organ, vessel, muscle, nerve, tissue, bone, and cell has specific capabilities and purpose. The physical being is meant to coordinate, communicate, and develop into a higher level of ability following predicted stages of growth.

Before we were born, we were designed. We are designed in the ethereal. Human life begins with conception at a cellular level of egg and sperm. From this microscopic miraculous formation, we develop and evolve. Conception begins a series of miraculous processes as unique strands of infinitesimal DNA weave complex codes, the blueprints to build our structure, sex, and interconnectedness. Everything is symmetrical, balanced, and woven by divine plan. There is nothing by chance or coincidence.

We develop and expand in intended order, with each division of growth increasing function and purpose. With each layer that is generated, the intricate complexities of our structure and connectedness—and how they relate to each other—are created. We are an immense web of messengers and receivers. Once our physical body is formed, consider the functions, coordination, communication, replication (such as hair and nails), and reconstruction (such as skin) of aspects of our body that happen continuously and extend our vitality and lifespan. Our divine plan includes road maps for the formation, growth, development, and equilibrium of our bodies. Even in our physical form, we are sacred beings.

"The body is a sacred garment. It's your first and last garment;
it is what you enter life in and what you depart life with,
and it should be treated with honor."

—Martha Graham

The mind is a complex system within the organ of the brain and our primary source of intelligence, communication, instruction, interpretation, storage, regulation, and maintenance for the body. Without a functioning mind we cannot survive independently. Through thinking, reasoning, and understanding, we determine our thoughts, behaviors, and actions. The brain is an organ of the body, comprised of dense tissue and matter, that conducts and transmits signals to stimulate actions. The mind, on the other hand, is the culmination of that connectedness, interpreting and instructing our body actively and passively, voluntarily and involuntarily, to optimize its collective reasoning.

Think of everything the mind does! The intelligence of the mind creates language, thinking, thoughts, reasoning, and feelings. It responds to what it senses. It processes and stores information and directs our actions. It affects body functions by responding to changes in temperature, hormones, fluid levels, electrolytes, system and chemical imbalances, and nerve impulses. It houses the ego, personality, judgments, and all functions of the psyche. It creates ideas, understanding, perceptions, imagination, and consciousness.

Thoughts are processes of energy transmission. Using the mind, we create ideas, feelings, and responses. We choose to envelop them, ignore them, or project them. Regardless of their source, thoughts give insight into our personality, life situations, and interpretation of states of happiness, challenge, fear, and emotion.

Emotions are the products of sensory perception. Sensory receptors transmit signals through our body to be interpreted by the mind. Emotions are powerful stimulators of feelings. Feelings embed impressions that influence the way that we react to sensory stimuli now and in the future.

Emotions are another dimension of self, an extension of our feelings, and an additional layer to mind, body, and spirit. Emotions bridge vibrational energy from mind to heart, where they can connect with spiritual energy. It is through emotion that we embody the physical and mindful aspects of the world to discover the meaning they hold for our lives. Emotions frequently override logic and objectivity. The release of past emotional patterns is essential in becoming an enlarged self, the self we are meant to be, the self we are asked to be.

Emotions can create embedded feelings that are hard to reframe. Remember that what you feel at one place in time may not be what you feel later based on your continued growth, maturity, and further experiences. The differences between feelings and emotions are subtle, and sometimes the words are interchanged. Feelings are usually associated with an experience, whereas emotions are based on a response to that experience. For instance:

* Feeling: "I felt lost and unsafe on my way into the city."
* Emotion: "I was so scared and afraid, I didn't know which way to turn."

You can see how this emotion might resurface the next time you are driving on unfamiliar roads in a city.

Emotions are very powerful. We can choose to react, suppress, or process them. Release of past emotional patterns is essential for our health and wellness. Think about how you emotionally respond or react to situations. How much is spontaneous, habitual, or ingrained?

How much is learned behavior or mimicking others?

Storage of negative emotions is a burden that you carry. It can lead to a large buildup over time, like a wall, a barricade. This accumulation of negative emotions can produce physical symptoms such as depression, malaise, aches, pains, and even forms of illness. It's hard to let go of emotional buildup. But why hang on to things that are not promoting your wellness, that are not helpful to you? Do they give you a false sense of protection, as if by storing them you will be prepared for a possible next time? Is it easier to feel and retain the emotional buildup than the loss of that perceived truth?

Understanding our emotions begins with a simple question: "Why do I feel this way?"

And then: "Does this feel right? Is there anything I wish to change?"

When a wave of emotion rises from within, accept it as being genuine and allow it to process. What you feel is what you interpret. What you feel is what you know. Center your mind, body, and spirit within your heart. Begin conscious breathing to release energy and open passageways for new thought to come forward. Visualize your heart space and its expansiveness. Embrace yourself with your loving arms, encircling the *all* of you. You are loved. You are safe. You are given the time you need to process all that comes forward. When you experience new peace and balance, you are ready to move on. Trust the guidance inside you to be the person you desire to be.

Journaling and exercise are wonderful ways to further process emotions. When I write in my journal to process something, I start my passage with questions like the previously stated: "What do I feel?"; "Why do I feel this?"; "Does this feel right or not right?"; "Is there something I'd like to change?" I keep writing responses to the questions until I cannot think of anything else. I write whatever comes to mind, and I don't try to analyze it. It is a work in progress. I write what comes to mind *even if I don't want to.*

Walking is my favorite form of exercise. I'm in nature—I see it, I feel it, and I breathe it in. I call on my angel team to accompany me and speak to me. I ask for their guidance and messages. I have a walking mantra that I repeat: "Relax, release, receive, replenish, breathe."

I repeat it as I walk until there are openings in which energetic messages can flow to me in words or thoughts for me to consider. These are thoughts to assist me in growth and expansion as long as I am open for this guidance to flow to me.

The mind stores memory and knowledge and is an important source of learning because it converts experiences into a perceived reality. These perceptions and inferences guide choices, communications, behaviors, and actions. In the earthly plane, we use our minds as a navigational tool to effectively manage the physical self. The mind is in the driver's seat. The body is the vehicle. Beyond ourselves, we can open our minds to receive guidance and messages from the flow of divine energy channeled to us. When we accept this limitless gift, the universe can assist us in envisioning and creating that which we desire.

"The shell must break before the bird can fly."

—Alfred, Lord Tennyson

Spirit is one with our higher self, the connection to light and love within us. Spirit is always present. Spirit is always open. Spirit connects with our soul and higher self through our heart so we may be one with all. Spirit is the life energy force that guides our journey and reveals all that is, all that has been, and all that will be. Spirit is our connection with holy. When we are one with Spirit, we are open to allow all messages and blessings to come forward. It is not from you; it is through you.

There are things we believe and things we know. "I believe" is an act of the mind. The phrase conveys a level of confidence, and, as a result, it generates a level of faith. There is an expectation that something will come forward, something directly related to our expressed belief.

"I know" is an act of the spirit. It does not come from mind or ego. "I know" comes from a higher place, a place of truth. To know is without doubt or distance. Knowing is finding your inner truth—the truth that has been trying to find you all your lifetimes. There are no expectations of knowing beyond its own truth.

"Earth's crammed with heaven."

—Elizabeth Barrett Browning, *Aurora Leigh*

Spiritual life within the vessel integrates mind, body, and spirit into one unifying form. As integrated beings, we are capable of discovering and knowing our truths and purpose.

Discovery Thoughts

Emotions create feelings that are processed through the mind. How do emotions affect your responses to life events?

....

What are things you believe in, have faith in? What do you expect in return for those beliefs?

....

Affirmation: "I live in truth. My spirit guides me to express my integrity and authenticity."

....

Now add an affirmative thought to continue your flow of positive energy: "I . . ."

....

Dimensions of Mind, Body, and Spirit

"Seek not outside yourself, heaven is within."

—Mary Lou Cook

The dimensions of the human self are vast. Each level adds depth to our ability to process and comprehend information and respond in our best interest. Levels of human growth occur in processes that move in an orderly fashion. Some steps may overlap with others, but they are all important in overall progress and achievement.

The art of balance, for example, is necessary to walk effectively, to ride a bicycle, and to dance. We know that increasing abilities to balance develop over time so that we can achieve more complicated movements, such as gymnastics. Developmental stages are not age specific, but can relate instead to stages of growth, such as infant, child, adolescent, and adult.

In other instances, we can skip over a step that we don't necessarily need to accomplish something. For example, some babies don't crawl before they walk. They may rock back and forth on their knees or scoot on their bottoms for weeks or months and then pull themselves up on the rung of a kitchen chair. From a standing position they begin their first teetering steps. They walk before they crawl. When they want to, they will go back and demonstrate that they can crawl (maybe following their brother's remote car toy) but it will be on their timeline and choosing. It is not necessary to crawl before you walk—crawling is only necessary to build strength, coordination, and balance.

Each level of growth builds on another. Each level brings with it intended learnings (knowledge, abilities, and understanding) that propel us to the next. These developmental stages have been studied and written about for centuries from physical, psychological, and behavioral viewpoints. We know as individuals that we grow and learn at our own pace while demonstrating progress moving forward.

"We cannot teach people anything;
we can only help them discover it within themselves."

—Galileo Galilei

In the body, everything is growing at the same time but at different rates of growth. Therefore, all aspects of our physical self reach levels of maturity at different times but are usually expected to be completed by adulthood, ages eighteen to twenty-one. This does not include continued learning and expansion from further experiences. Physically we are building organs, bones, muscles, blood vessels, cells, and all other components of our physical self while our brain (another organ of the body) begins to assimilate sounds and pictures that lead to communication and cognitive ability. The body is primarily a nurturing and sensing vehicle for our growth and maintenance. Initially this is a survival mechanism and then it is used to reach progressive levels of independence and mastery of abilities.

The mind is a complex communicator that receives information (sorts it), interprets it (sets priority, perceives negative and positive), relays it (takes action), and stores it (via memory and feelings). The growth of mindfulness leads us to discovery and connection with family, social sphere, and ourselves, and it can eventually lead to realization of our higher self and Spirit.

The awareness of positive and negative (the basis of truth) begins as parental and societal rules. Adults who oversee children (parents, teachers, clergy, and law enforcement) expect compliance. Reward or punishment from them solidifies our interpretation of right and wrong in the psyche, perhaps even for lifetimes. As the child gains increasing self-awareness and self-worth, independence and maturity, their own truth becomes more apparent. One's truth, or authenticity, forms within each individual as they determine the qualities they value in others and themselves. It is this "higher self" of one's authenticity that can bridge the heart space to connect with Spirit.

Spirit is a multi-dimensional energy that connects with higher self. We have the ability to expand our energy and connect beyond our physical self to other planes of vibrational energy, to the ethereal and the divine. Spirit is an energy receptor and transmitter, to us and from us, in many forms. We are blessed to receive its guidance and messages, which come to our mind in the form of words, symbols, and sensations. These are not limited by time, and they convey present, past, and future. Continued guidance and connection can be a source of enlightenment in our lives. Episodes of enlightenment broaden our awareness, insight, knowledge, and awakening as a divine being.

Everything we do as a divine being of light and love is some form of communication. We are, by design, meant to communicate. Think back upon your day and everything that occurred. You arose telling your body and mind it was time to start the day. Perhaps you interacted with people in your family. You put on a coat expecting it to be cool outside and drove in your car to complete a task. Your actions throughout the day tell others about your job, how you feel, and what you want. You eat to tell your body to nourish itself, and at the very end of your day, you turn to bed, telling your body it's time to rest. Every action, word, thought, posture, and facial expression is a form of communication. Communication is our gift to ourselves and to the world.

We exist in three planes of communication: communication with the self, connection from the self to others, and extension of ourselves beyond the self.

Communication
(with the Self, from the Self, beyond the Self)

Communication with the Self

"In your silence God's silence ceases."

—Paramahansa Yogananda

The mind is a vibrant wellspring of information, ideas, and thoughts waiting to be processed and conveyed. We communicate verbally, behaviorally, and creatively within ourselves and to others. What we communicate resonates within us and around us. Communication is the most important and complex ability that we have been blessed with.

Our ability to communicate is a developmental process that is ongoing throughout our lives. Communication is essential for learning and knowledge, relationships, development, and survival. It allows us to convey our needs, desires, and choices. It expands our awareness of ourselves, the environment, our world, and beyond. Our words express desires, needs, and feelings that create the environment we live in, the environmental soil we plant our seeds in. Communicating fully and effectively is essential to experience balance, harmony, and growth.

There are numerous ways the mind, body, and spirit communicate with us, with self. Communication is necessary to guide and facilitate our choices. Communication with the self builds personality, self-esteem, self-worth, and character—what we believe about ourselves. These beliefs are powerful impressions upon the mind and are fastidious in their hold on our psyche. The purpose of this communication is to help us experience well-being, balance, understanding, and authenticity. Benefits of honest communication include uniqueness (outwardly displaying personality and beliefs), trust in ourselves (internal value), and character (staying true to our values).

Communication can be verbal or nonverbal. We communicate to ourselves and others through language, sounds, signals, body movements, listening, and responding. Behaviorally, we are always communicating. Our expressions, actions, eye and hand movements, and body language all convey something. Our messages display thoughts, acceptance, rejection, and level of interest. Creatively we can express ourselves through dreams, ideas, thoughts, art, song, writing/journaling, and the decisions we make. We can indicate if we are receptive to change and working to create a new balance. Words and thoughts create our reality and the vibrational energy emanating from us.

The ego is a psychological extension of the mind that lives in the subconscious. Memory storage and instinctual frameworks (what you are prone to do) reside in the unconscious. According to Freud, the unconscious is the part of the psyche that influences thoughts and behaviors without the person's awareness. Personality uncovers itself in the conscious mind. Personality (the self we outwardly display) and self-esteem (the internal value we give ourselves) are powerful influences in decisions and growth. Like chains that secure us in a stationary pose, ego beliefs continuously feed themselves on what we attract and absorb, always resurrecting feelings of insecurity and fear to remain in power. Sometimes referred to as the shadow side, the ego tries to undermine our efforts to reveal our true selves. It is driven by its need for power. That's interesting, isn't it? That there is a part of us that strives for power, to always be in control. It is important when we're communicating with self that we understand our motives and what lies behind the words we choose, that we acknowledge the ego and how it influences us.

There are multiple ways in which we communicate with ourselves.

Senses begin to develop as part of the fetal growth process. Scientists have well documented the fetus's response to various stimuli: music, massage and caresses, and familiar voices, for example. Our senses serve to aid us in perceiving and interpreting. They guide us. Sight, smell, taste, touch, and hearing create messages and impressions that are interpreted by the mind. In this process, the physical connects with the mind. Interpretation of our senses strengthens our choices and understanding of the environment in which we live.

"Nothing can cure the soul but the senses,
just as nothing can cure the senses but the soul."

—Oscar Wilde, *The Picture of Dorian Gray*

Intuition, the sixth sense, is an inner guidance, a spirit-to-mind connection that guides us in many ways. It allows us to communicate with what is invisible in the physical world to reveal its meaning.

Free will is a state of internal balance that allows us to do, say, and think without constraints from external factors. When we exercise free will, we strengthen our personal power and our authenticity. Free will is not impulsive but is determined by the skills we have to analyze and make optimum decisions.

Instinct is our ability to physically and mindfully assess surrounding stimuli and respond without further reasoning. When we instinctually know something, our conscious and subconscious mind, including our memory, trigger an inherent response to what we perceive.

Choice is our ability to implement decisions that promote further action. Every choice is an opportunity to exercise personal freedom. Personal freedom is making choices and acting consciously in our best interest. The mind evaluates options based on knowledge, experience, and circumstances, and then determines the best choices to act upon. When we use this thought process, choices come from the conscious mind and are not influenced by fear, anger, pride, or emotions.

Emotions arise (from the heart) that have been processed by the sensory dimensions of awareness and perceptions of the mind. We choose how to process emotions with responses ranging from superficial to visceral, depending on the value and importance we place on the factors involved. We express emotions in many ways. These expressions may be overt or stifled, loud or silent, spontaneous or learned (repeating behavior). An emotional reaction can be released or can be retained as an impression on our conscious and subconscious mind. Any emotion we retain is embedded in memory and will try to resurface with similar experiences. Communicating and understanding our emotional responses is a process of growth that promotes maturity, internal balance, and healing.

Self-worth and self-esteem are interrelated and influence each other. We begin to develop both in early childhood. Self-worth comes from the expectations, the goals, we have for ourselves and our assessment of how well we meet them. Self-worth is a gradient value that we measure through our perceptions. Self-esteem comes from the respect and dignity we give ourselves based on our assessment of our performances and experiences in life—how well we achieve, how well we acquire and display abilities. The positive or negative feedback of others directly affects our self-esteem. Influenced and reinforced by such external factors, we judge our appearance, actions, and beliefs as good or bad, positive or negative. Positive experiences can build self-esteem while negative experiences may lower self-esteem. We wrestle internally with the need to be loved and accepted by others versus our own thoughts and free will. Our beliefs about ourselves reside in the conscious, subconscious, and ego mind. What we believe about ourselves dictates internal communication and our ability to optimally grow and develop. With further growth and understanding of truth and authenticity, self-worth and self-esteem become a connection of the higher self.

The inner child is the essence of our early childhood, our connection and communication with our earliest years and perhaps other lifetimes—our original true self, pure and genuine, before the influences of family, society, and ego. The inner child speaks to us of a time of beginning when we were free to be ourselves and we expressed desires and needs without reservation. We were naïve and pure in many ways. Connecting with your inner child may unlock suppressed needs and issues that weighed heavily on your development. Your inner child beckons you to reawaken the playful, innocent, adventurous younger self within you. They desire you to uncover, rediscover, and be the mature parent who understands them. The inner child lives in the subconscious mind but is not far from the surface of consciousness. If you desire to connect and rekindle that relationship, they will respond.

An exercise I recommend to all is to create a scrapbook that speaks to your inner child. It's fun and revealing! Use a clean notebook or journal with nothing else written in it. Start fresh. Enter the date and time of the start of your book. Jot down words that come to mind when you think of yourself as a young child: nouns, verbs, adjectives, nicknames, pet names, toys, dolls, games, sports, and stuffed animal names. Places you lived. Beds you slept in.

And feelings. What feelings emerge?

What questions come up? "Who am I? Who was I? Who do I want to be?"

Start looking through magazines and cut out pictures that reflect you and your memories. Do research on the internet for topics that describe you or your interests: sandcastles, jump rope, baking cookies. Print that page and cut out the pictures.

Sort your pictures and determine the order or flow you want to put them in. It could be what you remember chronologically based on places you lived or in order of your most favorite. You could sort by relationships with your parents, siblings, or other relatives and friends. Start to paste the pictures in the book.

Add descriptions or explanations as you feel necessary, as well as anything that comes to mind. Add things that represent your recollections but don't exactly match. For instance, a picture of any house might represent the first house you remember. Remember all those stairs? And you couldn't climb well!

Record things that you remember as being important—visual, auditory, olfactory. The beautiful flowers in the park, the smell of the ocean. Paste those pictures in your book.

Picture your inner child. How can you relate to them? What would you like to say? What would you like to ask? Picture yourself sitting on a front-porch step next to your inner child. In time, they will let you hold their hand or put your arm around them. How does that feel to you? It's been a long time. Rekindling relationships takes time.

It took me many weeks to create my inner child book, and I still go back and reread it and add to it. And I ask my inner child, "What would you like to tell me?"

The book is filled with pictures of dogs, dolls, bicycles, and beaches. I have a twin sister, and she is there too in recognition of the very important relationship we had and still have today. There are representations of the gardens that surrounded our home and cooking with my family. Pictures of things that connected me and made me feel loved.

As I ask questions, answers come to me when I walk or dream, and when I cut out more pictures. I ask, "What type of parent and friend would you want me to be for you? What could I give you that you need or never received?" Visualize yourself in situations where you are that adult person giving to the child in you. Put your arms around them, touch them, comfort them. Heal both of you.

There are seven main chakra energy points in the body from the top of the head to the base of the spine. They correspond to bundles of nerves, major organs, and areas of our energetic body that affect our emotional and physical well-being. Chakra energy balances our body and mind to integrate healing and to open ourselves to enlightenment. The energy of our chakras influences our health, decisions, and ability to connect to our higher self through the heart chakra. The practice of Reiki utilizes chakra energy to identify areas for healing. Chakra energy communication predominantly occurs on a subconscious level. Chakra energy is sometimes depicted within the Tree of Life as seven ascending branches conveying love and unity within all.

Dreams are the messages of our subconscious mind. These visions come to us as images, thoughts, and stories. They may arise from experiences, fears, or desires in the present, past, and future time. Dreams increase our awareness and are meant to guide us. You may or may not remember a dream or understand its meaning. Upon awakening from dreams, I would encourage you to write down any parts of them you remember. Over time their purpose may become more apparent. If you experience a moment of déjà vu, where you feel that you have been there before, look at your past experiences and see if anything is similar. Add your déjà vu experience to your dream log or journal.

"I've dreamt in my life dreams that have stayed with me ever after, and changed my ideas; they have gone through and through me, like wine through water, and altered the color of my mind."

—Emily Brontë, *Wuthering Heights*

Connection from the Self

We are innately, by design, social beings. Communication from self vibrates into the world around us intentionally and unintentionally. We build relationships, families, groups, and communities to relate to one another. We are attracted to others and thus wish to communicate with them. We desire to share and receive, develop and create, and experience a broader knowing of ourselves by knowing another person.

Our first efforts of communicating are smiles and gurgles, waving arms and legs. We are searching. We want acceptance and acknowledgment and something to be communicated back to us. Communication from self begins with physical movements and episodes of crying. Crying as an infant communicates needs: to be fed, changed, held, and nurtured. Crying is the universal language of the infantile. Crying in older years communicates both needs and emotions.

As we learn language and other forms of overt communication, we increase aspects of our personality and identity contained therein. We learn from feedback, especially adult feedback, that we are smart, cute, and funny or noisy, disruptive, and naughty. Whether truthful or not, these comments promote the development of further character traits. This type of feedback communication builds off foundational trust. We seek to better know ourselves by knowing another person.

From our body we can behave, act, and verbally and physically demonstrate to project our communication out into the world.

Language develops in complex ways, from sounds to words, sentences, telling stories, and creating ideas. Some children speak different languages from their early years, freely communicating from one style back to the other. Writing is the art of language. Writing unlocks the secret door to expression and the treasure chest of reading. Language is the predominant form of communication we use in our lives.

Our outward communications, such as words, expressions, mannerisms, physical connection, gestures, avoidance, and aggressiveness, display our intent and can be an invitation or a barrier to others. Whatever we communicate is a form of energy and will elicit a response. We can display openness in allowing the flow of communication to move outward and then return, or we can model body language that blocks its circulation. Our communication can invite others forward or turn them away.

From our mind we can think and verbalize what we believe and desire. Thoughts and ideas are prevalent forms of mindful communication. Imagination takes thoughts to a higher level of expression that does not need to be understood or proven. We use our minds to organize and prioritize communication that aligns us with a purpose and goals. Through thoughts and words, we create a path of intended steps to reach expected outcomes.

We manifest content and create affirmative steps aligning us with intended outcomes. When we communicate from the mind, we project energy out into the universe. This creates movement leading to actions. This action may or may not be returned to us. In other words, we may not be aware of what we create through our mindful communication. Ultimately, however, we are responsible for what we create.

Conscious listening is a form of silent communication. Listening allows others to share and release their opinions and needs and allows us to gain insight into their world and daily life. Our purpose is not to respond but to absorb and relate to the person and the information. Conscious listening evokes compassion and is a very powerful way of gaining understanding and building relationships.

From our spirit we connect with our higher self and Spirit through prayer, meditation, and expansion beyond the three-dimensional world. Our spiritual self thrives on communication. Prayer is the simple language of the heart that is open to the outward flow of energy and the inflow of energy in the form of grace. The universe guides expressed energy to its highest good. Our role is not to navigate it but to share it and trust. Communication with Spirit increases our awareness of self and soul purpose. This relationship unveils the truths we are open to receiving as well as authenticity, the truth of ourselves. As in all relationships, frequent honest connection with our spiritual self is key to its evolution and expansion.

Extension of Ourselves Beyond the Self

"I am rooted, but I flow."

—Virginia Woolf, *The Waves*

All communication is an energy form. Whether we are thinking or saying or moving, our actions generate and transmit energy. We have the capabilities to transmit and receive energy beyond the traditional three-dimensional world. This includes to and from other physical selves, other living things, and those in the angelic and ethereal realm. Beyond ourselves, communication exceeds a 3D reality. The universe and Spirit continuously transmit energy in the form of guidance and messages to us.

Why do we communicate in this way? Are we special? Are we hearing and seeing this communication because we are different from others? No, not different, just open to hearing. Open to discover, to know, and to understand that which lives beyond ourselves. Think about it: You are extending an invitation to connect with the forces that guide you. Communication may come to you as a nagging voice inside or a thought that just won't go away. These guiding messages seek to enhance your life.

With growth and openness, we learn how to listen, hear, and

interpret these messages, and from there we choose. You may choose to listen or not, to follow the guidance or not, to explore your gifts more fully or not. You may choose that you're just not going to listen anymore. You're done. It's okay. You can take a break. Your energy connection is a dynamic that is always with you. Just because you choose to ignore this ability does not make it go away. There will be other opportunities, many other opportunities. The universe and Spirit continuously transmit energy through guidance and messages.

Some people have attributes that help them communicate beyond the self. A clairsentient, for example, is a person who can sense the energy of a location, a person, or an object through the mind. They are apt, for example, to know which way to go to find a restaurant without looking at a map, using the information coming to them. These are the people who can find a lost child by following the energetic guidance coming to them.

A clairaudient can hear internal or external vibrational messages on a different level of transmission. They perceive what is inaudible to others, such as music playing or voices.

A claircognizant receives and interprets information through intrinsic knowledge as it flows to their mind. This information can relate to the past, present, or future, and may only partially reveal a situation.

Energy and vibrational communication can also be described as a process, as in the following. For example, telepathy is a form of extrasensory perception (ESP). It is an ability to transfer and/or receive thoughts through means other than the five senses. Telepathy may be referred to as intuition, channeling, or clairvoyance.

Transmission is the ability to silently message thought and energy for the purpose of enhancing life. Reiki is an example of transmission where positive energy flows from the hands of the practitioner above the client's body to promote balance and wellness. I attended a workshop once where we were taught how to send energy to others through our breathing. The speaker used this method to relieve his wife's depression. By focusing on the person and exhaling through an open mouth (as if you were going to whistle), you send energy to help release the person's blocked energy. In my experience, the recipient can sometimes feel this like a slight breeze on the back of their neck.

Transcendence is an experience of consciousness beyond the physical level, beyond the limitations we associate with physical reality. People may describe this as an out-of-body experience. As an intensive care nurse, I have had the privilege to witness transcendence several times. The patient appears to have died, and the monitors do not show a pulse or breathing. In a relatively short period of time, however, they awaken and tell stories of what is on "the other side." I have also had critically ill patients who say that there are people in the room talking with them. These are people I could never see but were later explained by family as relatives and friends who had previously passed.

Ascension is the process by which we elevate consciousness to achieve higher dimensional understanding and function. We experience aspects of awakening, purifying, releasing, and rebirth as we rise, through which we proceed to be one in unity with all life and divine life. The most profound example apparent to me in my lifetime is Mother Teresa. By her service to God in all her actions, she was an example of the ascension process, culminating in sainthood. Components of the ascension processes can occur in all of us throughout our lifetime based on our chosen purpose and life path. Ascension before death is related to our rise in consciousness, with increasing levels to be one with higher self and Spirit. At the time of death, each of us experiences the highest level of ascension on Earth where in soul form we energetically rise to be one with Spirit.

In summary, our abilities to communicate occur on three levels (with self, from self, and beyond self) and depend on our capabilities and surrounding environment. All communication involves vibrational energy transmission and allows us to extend ourselves beyond a physical dimension.

Using the dimensional models and guideposts described in this chapter, think of how you have experienced greater communication and connection. Think of your journey as a never-ending life process and know that what you aspire to be and do is within your capabilities. It is all only a thought away.

"From the beginning I had a sense of destiny, as though my life was assigned to me by fate and had to be fulfilled. This gave me an inner security, and, though I could never prove it to myself, it proved itself to me. I did not have this certainty, it had me."

—Carl Jung

We have multiple ways within ourselves of interpreting and processing energy communication and extensive ways of extending ourselves beyond our physical being. The powers of energy communication and transmission allow us to expand in all dimensions of mind, body, and spirit. We are whole in our self-discovery when we are open to explore all that exists in the world around us and within us.

Discovery Thoughts

Communication with self is very personal. How does your internal communication promote your growth?

....

All relationships are built upon communications from self and reflect the wholeness of mind, body, and spirit. How honestly and openly do you feel you communicate with others?

....

How have you experienced communication beyond yourself? What do you believe was the purpose? How did you respond?

....

Affirmation: "I embrace my self-discovery. Communication leads me to expansion."

....

Now add an affirmative thought to continue your flow of positive energy: "I ..."

....

Chapter 4

One with Spirit

*"Everyone has a special purpose, a special talent or gift to give to others,
and it is your duty to discover what it is. Your special talent is
God's gift to you.
What you do with your talent is your gift to God."*

—Gautama Chopra

Growth occurs in all places of our lives and in all dimensions. It is limitless. If we try to quantify and measure it, we focus on the physical aspects that the ego mind uses to compare us with all things.

As human beings, it is common for us to compare ourselves with other humans. This primarily occurs in physical and mindful comparisons: intelligence, strength and motor abilities, physical characteristics, and how we view others in our relationships. Part of this comparison may help us to achieve a higher level of functioning; for instance, in athletics we might strive to run faster or longer than someone else to win races and hold records. The other part of this comparison, however, is the ego mind that seeks to prove we are better than someone else. Our insecurities use comparison to determine if we are better or not. "Better" is another way of saying "more powerful."

Continuing to move forward in trust, exploring that which is before us, we walk our soul path with higher self. In the spiritual world there is no definition of "better." It is not needed. We create what we intend. We are as we choose, and we change as we desire. Know that you are blessed and guided in all ways to live your life to its fullest.

In the Soul Garden, our refuge and sanctuary, we can see without judgment. We can know the truth of what we have created to confidently move forward and continue to pursue our life purpose.

In the garden, we are one with Spirit in energy form. The Soul

Garden *is* a Garden of Eden that we create as a unique, beautiful reflection of the eternity of our soul. As divine beings we create a sanctuary that speaks to us as an individual. We desire to create a refuge, a space where the burdens of the physical world will not constrain us, nor limit us in fully experiencing the universal world we live in. The Soul Garden is a state of endless freedom and enlightenment.

The Higher Self

*"I learned that the real creator was my inner self, the Shakti. . . .
That desire to do something is God inside talking through us."*

—Michelle Shea

The higher self is the connection to Spirit from our physical being. It is an aspect of ourselves that unites our energy and understanding in the earthly world with the spiritual world. The higher self is our most authentic elevated form of consciousness. In this state of consciousness and energy connection, we can be one with Spirit.

The higher self knows where you have been, where you are, and where you are meant to be. It knows the choices you have made and the paths you have walked. It is always seeking balance and alignment with soul energy, guiding you to a state of well-being and eternal love. Through this place of alignment and enlightenment, answers to questions that are challenges or obstacles to our well-being become apparent. Thoughts and messages support our growth and balance. The higher self seeks to show you the answers to the questions that are always within you.

Unlike the Tree of Life, our higher self does not embody karma. As such, the higher self reveals options that are present to consider without influence or past constraints. The higher self in conjunction with Spirit seeks the best possible outcomes for our life and for our highest good. It speaks in truth and wisdom in the present from connection with the divine and the universe.

Dimensions of Oneness

"Your capacity to be fully present expands dramatically when you stop identifying yourself as a time-bound human being separate from others, and start experiencing life as a timeless spiritual being at one with all creation."

—Phil Bolsta

Oneness with Spirit is a state of being. In living your life on Earth, you are in a constant state of being that is influenced and morphed with changing circumstances. To "be" means to simply exist. Therefore, your state of being describes the quality and state of that existence. A state of being is made up of qualities and not life goals.

A state of *being* is not to be confused with a state of *mind*. Your state of being describes yourself within your current environment and circumstances in life. Your state of mind describes your perceptions and emotions, particularly what you're feeling at a moment in time.

The level with which your physical being can recreate dimensions of oneness with Spirit is proportional to your consistency of living in divine light and love. In other words, the purity with which you live your life impacts your ability to be open, to share, and to live in eternal love. The following seven states of being—dimensions of our oneness—are embedded in the Soul Garden and reflected in all that grows within you and from you. Once we experience these states of being, we are then able to bring them into the earthly plane through Spirit's connection with our higher self, and then to our mind as we adopt them.

States of Being

Serenity: A State of Being

"Everything has its wonders, even darkness and silence, and I learn, whatever state I may be in, therein to be content."

—Helen Keller

"Serenity" is a lovely word, a lovely feeling, a lovely image. We are the creators of our own serenity in all that we plant and nurture in the Soul Garden. You are your Soul Garden. You are the life that plants seeds, nourishes growth, and blooms in spiritual presence. Your garden reflects what has been, is now, and what will be. As a gardener of your sacred soil, you are the guardian for its well-being and what it brings forth. Your garden exists as you exist. Your garden thrives as you thrive. Your garden replicates the light and love you bring into the world.

Serenity as a state of being breeds acceptance and peace. This is not to say that everything in our physical life is always positive and calm. We process events, analyze them, and store them. What we store affects our state of serenity.

We know when our life is not serene. Negative feelings loom over us like a dark cloud. Stress, for example, is a sensation we embody in response to circumstances we feel are overwhelming. Its effects can range from despair to anger, from vulnerability to determination. Over time stress creates issues with health and wellness. At its basis, stress is akin to fear of losing control as we strive and struggle to maintain superiority above the circumstances we live with.

We would like to feel better, but we don't know how. Stress misleads us to believe that if we were just *more* than what we are, we could master the current circumstances. Ego rules our desire for control and all aspects of being *more*. It is especially hard to gain serenity if we are not willing to release the burdens of negative feelings and emotions and instead choose to hold on to them like a badge of courage because we were "right" or we want to show others that we survived as "innocent victims." If you have ever experienced this you may add, "And I wore the badge proudly!" Maybe for a moment in time that was true and maybe feeling justified even helped you cope in some way, but just like our need for power, the need to feel justified can consume us.

Early on we are taught that there are two choices: right and wrong. If you are right, you are a good child. If you are wrong, you are a bad or naughty child. Being right about how you feel validates your emotions. If you are not "right" then it often feels like criticism and judgment directed at you (by you). *There you are again, you naughty child.*

Serenity, however, is an environment of neutrality and equilibrium. Higher self requires higher perspective. Serenity unifies equilibrium with tranquility in all living things, source energy (Spirit), and our soul's purpose. In this place of high-frequency energy, you are in harmony with your own truth.

It is hard to live in a constant state of serenity, but we do yearn for it. Your inner voice, the higher self, reminds you to align whenever you start to drift away. When you are in the garden, observe the beauty that surrounds you and breathe in the purity and freshness of life. The life you are meant to have.

The garden abounds with your growth. In the garden, everything exists as we have created it. The garden is not affected by the external circumstances that impact us in the physical world. As a state of being, serenity creates wholeness by promoting peace in our life and our mind.

Bless your family for their relationship gifts to you. Be thankful for life's experiences, the people and events that have assisted you in becoming who you are. Express gratitude for those who give of themselves each day to bring food to your table, shelter to your body, and love into your life. Know that you are only who you are as a result of them, and as a result of all beings and things you connect with. I do not know the meaning of life as much as I know all life has meaning. We are a part of the magnificence of creation.

"The truth is that the inner Self of every human being is supremely great and supremely loveable. Everything is contained in the Self. The Divine Principle that creates and sustains the world pulsates within us as our own Self. It scintillates in the heart and shines through all our senses."

—Swami Muktananda

Discovery Thoughts

Picture yourself sitting in your Soul Garden under the Tree of Life, observing all you have created. What do you see that brings you a feeling of serenity?

....

How do you manage stressful situations that occur in your life? Is there something that creates stress in your life, something you would like to release the need for control over?

....

Affirmation: "I am the serenity of my garden. I bring peace to my life and into the world."

....

Now add an affirmative thought to continue your flow of positive energy: "I . . ."

....

"Spirituality is not a formula; it is not a test. It is a relationship. Spirituality is not about competency; it is about intimacy. Spirituality is not about perfection; it is about connection."

—Mike Yaconelli

The following serenity exercise is a wonderful visualization to process any negativity, including burdens you have absorbed throughout your life.

* Find a place of repose—quiet, calm, relaxing. There is no need to rush.

* Close your eyes and refresh yourself. Take three big breaths, slowly in and out. Clear any thoughts that are interrupting you.

* You are by the ocean. Do you hear it? You can feel the sun on your face, and a slight wind brings the smell of salty air to you. Breathe it in. You can hear seagulls cawing above. They fly overhead and sway in the wind, swaying with the clouds, swooping down and then up, lifted as you and they are lifted higher.

* You move forward in the sand toward the sound of the waves, the rhythm repeating over and over, forward and back, lapping at the shore.

* Imagine you are barefoot. You are walking on the beach along the water's edge. The water caresses your toes. You like that feeling, that knowing, because it reminds you where you are.

* There is no need to rush. You can leisurely walk here. You are safe.

* The waves are turning, continuing their chant over and over. Let the repetition remind you of the continuum of each minute, each hour, each day.

* The life events we experience are like the waves coming to shore, some more forceful than others. Sometimes they take you by surprise and you stumble a bit. Then you regain your footing, breathe out, and the wave retreats.

* The tide leaves a faint white foam that dissolves into the sand, nothing else. Your toes are being washed again as the tide comes back. Walk forward now.

* The waves are the process of equilibrium that help remind us of a state of serenity. Regardless of the size of the waves coming in, they peak, begin to ebb, and carry away any remnants of fear and negativity. They wash away all that is no longer needed, all that does not serve a purpose in maintaining higher-self alignment.

* All that is no longer needed has been washed away. Your mind is clear and open as you experience the serenity now within you.

Alignment: A State of Balance

"Learn to get in touch with the silence within yourself and know that everything in this life has a purpose."

—Elisabeth Kübler-Ross

Balance, and therefore the capability to align, is essential in all our activities. It is an active process. We are continually adjusting to achieve symmetry and stability with the energy that encircles us. This energy comes from people, situations, work, responsibilities, challenges, and events occurring in our lives and on the Earth. Physically, our spine and protected spinal cord creates a connection point for all right and left limbs and structure to support the head and functions of the brain. This keeps our physical self in structural alignment.

Everything we do demands that our body, mind, emotions, and spirit are positioned so that we are able to optimally function at the highest level possible. Alignment transports the energy of our daily lives so it can be processed to meet our higher self and spirit. You are at the center of your vortex, with life's concentric rings circling outside of your energetic space. You choose what to absorb and what to allow to be its own entity. Your balance is internal and not reliant on other energy or energy states to be whole.

To align is unification. To be unified is to experience a pleasing and consistent whole. When you align, you are detaching from your personal self, the ego self, to create a higher level of vibrational frequency within you.

"Just remain in the center; watching. And then forget that you are there."

—Lao Tzu

Your body and mind will always tell you when you are not in alignment. Being out of alignment feels like being on a road that stops before your destination because you can no longer see choices ahead, leaving you bewildered as to where to go next. When you can't go forward, you must back up.

I changed majors in college several times and for various reasons. I started in English because I wanted to pursue my writing until my father was adamant that I could not make a living being an "unpredictable" writer. I had to make a choice quickly before the next semester. I love people and especially children, and so I decided to move to social work, thinking I would eventually earn my master's degree and become a licensed social worker (LSW). But the division of social welfare lost its accreditation the next year. Deadlines set in for number of credits and type of degree required as far as getting into graduate school and I panicked. I jumped the guardrail and started moving north to the College of Life Sciences and a degree in child behavior and development (literally north, as that building was on the other side of campus). Most of my credits moved with me, and I graduated within the four years by taking additional courses for the remainder of the terms. Big breath! But then the road detoured again. Because I was married (that's a different story of balance and alignment), I chose not to move to Boston and begin work on my master's degree. Instead, I accepted enrollment in the School of Nursing at the university. I didn't want to be a nurse, but I thought I could use the degree to work as a resource support person with children within a hospital setting. When I received my nursing degree I saw the road ahead of me more clearly with every hospital experience. Being an RN brought together all my education, skills, and experiences into the one role I had hoped for. I accepted each position with open arms.

You cannot change the energy coming toward you, but you can modify it with changes in thoughts and activity. Being mindful of decisions and actions by listening, observing, and detaching (being consciously aware) creates an opportunity for aligning with higher self. This includes leaving people and situations that are harmful to your well-being. Bless them, bless the situation for the experience it brought to you. To be whole with higher self and the universe is an upward alignment within you and from you. The law of attraction reminds us that we attract what we think, say, and do, like a magnet pulling life force energy within. Everything we do is an opportunity to honor ourselves, and by doing so, we honor others.

> *"One's first step in wisdom is to question everything—*
> *and one's last is to come to terms with everything."*
>
> —Georg C. Lichtenberg

Discovery Thoughts

What practices and processes do you use to maintain balance in your life?

....

How do you center yourself and align with higher self?

....

Affirmation: "I am balanced and centered. I align with soul energy."

....

Now add an affirmative thought to continue your flow of positive energy: "I . . ."

....

Flow: A State of Allowing

"When I am silent, I fall into that place where everything is music."

—Rumi

Allowing is a state of surrender, yielding to the flow of divine energy to direct and guide you. When we believe in the universal flow of good, we can release fears and believe that all situations are intended for their highest good. With grace we gain the capacity to transcend matters transpiring at the personal level and see beyond the illusion of circumstances and emotions to a deeper truth.

I was very moved when I discovered the true meaning of surrender, the ultimate allowing. I was in the midst of adulthood and my career and very much used to approaching my life challenges head-on, as confrontation. I was determined to succeed, both in my nursing career and my role as a mother raising three children by myself. As I type these words the situation sounds formidable. But that is the truth of desperately needing control: The path is formidable. Control brings confrontation when we view forces as opponents we must square off against.

Back then, I relied on my willpower and personal drive to move me forward. Indeed, these actions created movement, but they only brought me to my knees time and time again.

The word "surrender" always evoked feelings of weakness in me, and I learned early in life not to show weakness—meaning, don't ask for help and don't cry. Instead, I was determined to be *strong, resilient*, and *persistent*. I now know these words have no relationship to the true meaning of surrender. As Marianne Williamson so articulately describes, "To the ego mind, surrender means giving up. To the spiritual mind, surrender means giving in and receiving."

I was so blessed not only to read her quote in my hours of need, but to embody its truth. Allowing is the key to receiving.

We open, allow, accept, receive.

We open our minds, allow Spirit to come forward, accept its intrinsic goodness, and receive it into our heart.

We know that when we are open, when we allow the universal flow of energy to freely flow, it will create movement for the highest good. It is not from you, but through you.

Allowing is not always easy. In the face of adversity our fight-or-flight instinct kicks in and thoughts of how to defend ourselves—defend our power—come to the forefront. In allowing, you realize that universal energy flow must be unobstructed. That means that you must free yourself from being attached to the dynamics of the process. You must free yourself from determining a solution, a predetermined outcome that you feel is acceptable.

Flow brings next steps forward and solutions you may not have even imagined. All of it is meant for your highest good, and the highest good of all. The key I was missing in my own circumstances was *trust*.

I experienced my awakening to flow and surrender in the same situation. My second son was born with a significant hearing deficit and did not even have a startle reflex. Here was this beautiful infant with wide eyes watching in a silent world. His pediatricians monitored this, and at eighteen months they sent us to an audiologist for him to undergo hearing testing. By this time, he was an active boy, and I had developed hand signals to accompany my words to direct him. I opened my arms wide for a hug and motioned with my hands for him to come forward. I mimicked what I wanted him to do. He responded so well I was sure he had some level of hearing. But that was not the case, and not the truth to his well-being.

From there we were sent to Children's Hospital of Philadelphia where the doctors felt he would greatly benefit from hearing aids. In fact, they wanted to surgically place hearing implants into his ears, a new technology that was highly superior to traditional hearing aids in transmitting sounds. Because of his rate of growth, these implants would need to be changed twice a year.

In the 1980s health insurance did not cover this procedure. I was working part-time in the ICU at a local medical center. I prayed with my whole heart to be shown how to afford this. I could work full-time. I could work two jobs. I prayed to be shown how to pay for this so that my son could have what he needed to hear.

My son was evaluated several times as an outpatient, and then we finally arrived on the day of surgery. One last test to make sure they had fine-tuned the technical intricacies of the implants to his utmost benefit. We sat in a soundproof room, my son in my lap, while the medical staff projected different sound frequencies into the room from different vantage points. We had done this several times before with no response from my son. Once again, there was no response . . . until there was.

He covered his ears and looked all around following the sounds! His head darted from one corner of the room to the next. I didn't know what was happening. The staff didn't know what was happening. But it did happen. He was hearing!

As you can imagine, there was much joy in the room, in the department, in this, the miracle. It was a miracle! I was speechless.

But here is my lesson in flow and allowing.

I had prayed for a way that I could afford the hearing aids for my son. My thoughts were focused on my attempt to control the situation. How could I provide for it? But it was only by the grace of God that my son received the gift of hearing.

Surrender means giving in and receiving.

That doesn't mean that we won't experience resistance as we try to open to the flow and allow. Resistance is a messenger telling us that actions are moving us forward. We gain traction with resistance to create time and space for us to reexamine our purpose and remain open to the flow of energy. Resistance heralds progress and a time to reassess, realign, and gather strength. We are fortified by resistance.

Flow allows us to confer energy upon something with conscious thought and positive intention. In manifestation we are conferring mindful energy upon a thought to visually magnify it into form. When we bless something, we are conferring spiritual energy upon it, setting an intention in the highest good.

"Everything in life that we really accept undergoes a change. So suffering must become love. That is the mystery."

—Katherine Mansfield

To be present and become one with the flow of energy, of life, we must open, allow, accept, and receive, being present to the evolving wisdom and guidance that is contained therein.

Discovery Thoughts 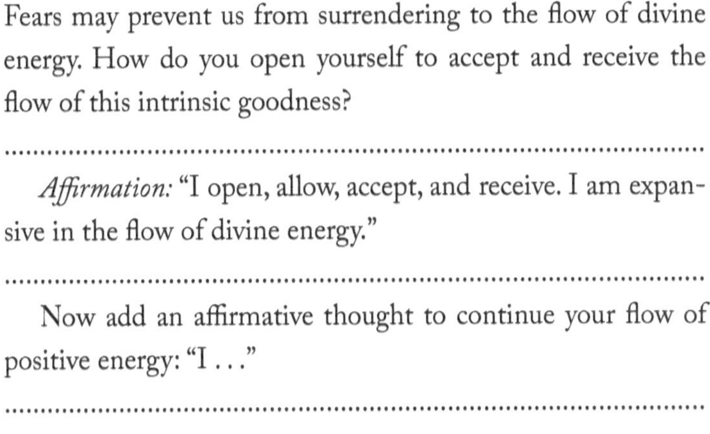

Fears may prevent us from surrendering to the flow of divine energy. How do you open yourself to accept and receive the flow of this intrinsic goodness?

....

Affirmation: "I open, allow, accept, and receive. I am expansive in the flow of divine energy."

....

Now add an affirmative thought to continue your flow of positive energy: "I ..."

....

Faith: A State of Belief

"You are not living by human laws. Expect miracles and see them take place. Hold ever before you the thought of prosperity and abundance and know that doing so sets in motion forces that will bring it into being."

—Eileen Caddy

Faith is a state of belief, and through that belief there is increased awareness and acceptance of life circumstances. Faith acknowledges that what is present at any given time is part of a greater process, a process blessed beyond our imagination or vision. We trust and hope that our prayers will be answered, knowing that all things occur for our highest good. Faith opens our mind to receive resources that are available to us, those that are tangible and intangible. Faith calms worries and fears and restores balance and peace of mind.

In the guidebook from *The 22 Archangels Oracle* card deck, Kyle Gray tells us that Archangel Faith is part of a holy trinity of angels with Charity and Hope. Her personal mission is to help us develop a trusting bond with our higher power so that we can live a life that's filled with purpose: "Trust in your ability to create miracles—the impossible is becoming possible."

Faith and I have become very close friends. Over the past decades of my many life changes and deteriorating physical conditions, I have experienced severe debilitating pain, paralysis, and multiple surgeries. All these experiences have strengthened and solidified my faith. There have been many dark times and depressive times. I came to think of my sadness as my shadow side. I visualized my feelings planted in my shade garden with roots always searching for the light. I would retreat there to find solace. I saw the plants growing in convoluted, overgrown ways, but their leaves were works of art. I could see the plants from a place above them and knew there was always light to help me and reassure me.

Faith opens us to optimism and hope. To see beyond where we are to what we believe will be better—a situation, a relationship, a place. Hope strengthens our conviction and helps us activate intentions and beliefs that all things are possible. We expect there will be changes in answer to our requests and prayers.

"Learn to wish that everything should come to pass exactly as it does."

—Epictetus

Faith brings *knowing* forward. Remember knowing? To say "I know" is an act of the spirit. To know is an embodiment of truth without doubt or distance. Knowing is finding your inner truth.

Knowing that God exists in all situations, we are never alone or abandoned. The act of faith creates a bond that solidifies us with purpose knowing that every occurrence is purposeful. It leads to a destination from which we can make other choices. With faith we believe in something greater than ourselves.

Here is faith's answer in your Soul Garden as you retrace your paths and review your plantings: All things are possible. Change is a process in one direction or another that leads to something. Change is not a permanent answer. If you continue to walk forward, you are creating energetic movements that activate other advancements. Faith assures us that all things are in process, and in divine order and divine timing.

Walk forward. You are never alone.

Discovery Thoughts

Take a moment to consider your present life circumstances. In faith, what do you believe will come forward?

....

Affirmation: "I live in faith. With faith I activate all intentions to their highest good."

....

Now add an affirmative thought to continue your flow of positive energy: "I . . ."

....

Love: A State of Communion

"All are but parts of one stupendous whole,
whose body Nature is, and God the Soul."

—Alexander Pope, "An Essay on Man: Epistle I"

All living things are created from the love of God, our divine creator. "Love" is a word that has been documented since the earliest forms of communication. Its ancient root is also the source of the Latin word "libido" or "desire." Throughout time the meaning of love has expanded its usage to incorporate more modern applications, especially in literature and theater: "Love is blind," for instance, and "For the love of the game." Love's most sincere meaning is in relation to the heart, the center of our being and connection to higher self and Spirit.

Love exists in many forms: compassion, kindness, communication, and touch. We describe numerous acts of kindness and compassion as loving. Yes, love in its truest sense is an expression of giving. Love is also allowing yourself to receive the love that is given to you. Behind a declaration of love to another, a bond forms between people. Once said, it cannot be taken lightly, dismissed, or forgotten.

The physical self—body, mind, and emotion—understands love and accepts love in a series of steps: growth, experience, and expansion. Age and maturity give variation and depth to our feelings and awareness of what we call love. We develop expectations. We understand love on deeper and progressive levels. We desire to love and be loved.

Love is a process of evolution, of unfolding, like the blossoms of a flower. Agape, or unconditional love, is the selfless expression of love outward without expectation of return.

The fourth chakra energy center is located in our heart space and is the energy bridge between the physical self (body and mind) and the spiritual self. In her book *Anatomy of the Spirit*, Caroline Myss describes the fourth chakra as "the central powerhouse of the human energy system. The middle chakra, it mediates between the body and spirit and determines their health and strength. . . . The chakra embodies the spiritual lesson that teaches us how to act out of love and compassion and recognize that the most powerful energy we have is love. Love is Divine Power."

The soul only knows and understands love. It will only grow love. The love we share and what we receive can be magnified beyond our understanding, beyond our dreams. Love of yourself. Love as a gift to others. Self-love, being accepting of yourself and the love of others toward you. To be able to love fully you must love yourself.

This is a priority and necessity.

Touch is the physical connection of one being to another that can be given and received as an act of love. We begin to learn about love at tender ages, embedding these learnings in our hearts and minds. With these childhood experiences the seeds of understanding self-love are sown. Feeling worthy and being valued allow us to trust and open ourselves to give and receive love and accept God's love for us.

"I have listened to the realm of the spirit.
I have heard my own soul's voice, and I have remembered
that love is the complete and unifying thread of existence."

—Mary Casey

In the eyes of love, we are all equal. In the eyes of love, we are all one in unity. Love has no boundaries.

We must love ourselves to truly love others. We must embrace sensitivity and kindness to understand our needs and accept who we are. To care for yourself with love is a generous gesture that elevates your capacity to love all.

Love is also a healing force of energy. To feel another's circumstances and emotions is a benevolent gift of love that sends hope and healing into their lives. You must nurture with love. Love plants seeds.

"The most important thing in life is to learn how
to give out love and how to let it come in."

—Morrie Schwartz

Grace, the gift of benevolence, is God's unconditional love. Through Spirit, each of us is made in his image, unique and gifted.

The love of our creator exists irrespective of our love for him. What we need we are able to receive. What we receive we are able to magnify. Grace blesses us to share, to embrace and release, and to give for the benefit of humankind, nature, and our Earth.

Love as a communion connects us to all people and all circumstances. By design, it is intended to be freely given to nurture, support, and elevate ourselves and others.

Love is the greatest gift we have been blessed with.

Discovery Thoughts

Picture yourself as the beautiful sacred being you are. How do you practice self-love?

....

Think about all the dimensions of love in your life. How have you experienced love as a healing force?

....

Affirmation: "My love is limitless. Grace blesses me with communion for all living things."

....

Now add an affirmative thought to continue your flow of positive energy: "I . . ."

....

Prayer: A State of Grace

"Prayer is not asking. It is a longing of the soul. . . . It is better in prayer to have a heart without words than words without a heart."

—Mahatma Gandhi

All thoughts are a form of prayer. Prayer is talking with God, our higher power, connecting us spiritually with love and unity, connecting us with all there is.

We pray to express, to connect, to ask for wisdom and guidance, to give thanks, to request for ourselves and others, to share, and to know God. We pray to attain what is beyond us, what is only attainable with the reach of the divine.

In prayer, sometimes we ask, sometimes we listen, and sometimes we give ourselves by offering to be of service. In affirmation, we express gratitude for our gifts. In appreciation, we give thanks for things that are coming forward and for those already present. Prayer is faith in process. All prayers, whether we say them aloud or silently, whether we are kneeling or driving in the car, are sacred.

When we commune with God we share from our hearts. We focus on God, not ourselves, and know that in his divine wisdom and timing all is abundantly coming forward. We give thanks for all there is and know that all that will be is as well.

*"Finally, I looked into my own heart and there
I saw Him; He was nowhere else."*

—Rumi

All thought is a form of prayer, a conversation through the mind to our higher self and Spirit. In prayer we create reflection and connection that poses our questions and heartfelt desires. In the quietness of a stilled heart space, we are supported in all ways. When we offer love and faith, we receive blessings in bountiful ways we could never imagine. We know that the grace of God blesses us. Carolyn Myss tells us that "grace is the breath of God." Breathe that in. Let it fill you.

Offering a blessing to someone is a prayer. When you do not know what to say, offer a blessing. When you witness the unfortunate, pain, or destruction, offer a blessing. The simplest prayer that I know is "Help. Help me, help them." Whether you say it for yourself or for others, it is without attachment and opens channels for grace to come forward.

Prayer has no requirements to place, time, or actions. Prayers to God, the universe, the creator, and all the angels are heard. Explanations are not required. The power of prayer transmits between all dimensions.

All prayers are answered. They are answered for the highest good of all in divine order and divine timing—perhaps not always in the way we anticipate but in a way that supports us and leads us onward. Divine answers move things forward. Trust that answers are occurring even if you don't see the results. Everything is in process one step at a time.

"The power in committing something to prayer comes not when I make a request, but when I release my attachment to the outcome."

—Daily Word Magazine

Joan Chittister, in her monthly publication *The Monastic Way*, tells us that "we do not pray in order to control God. We pray in order to become new within ourselves, to see differently, to see right. . . . Prayer simply opens us to God. After that, everything in life becomes the presence of God to us."

We become new with prayer as we are blessed with enlightenment. In the Soul Garden you walk the paths of what has been, what is, and what will be. As you walk in the garden, be present as an enlightened being. Open yourself to the journey and the vision.

Prayer illuminates our paths and creates opportunity. Prayer is the North Star, the guiding light. Prayers strengthen our service to live in union with all living things and to continue to seek our purpose on Earth.

In a state of grace, prayer becomes an act of love and gratitude. All thought is prayer connecting us with our higher self, with Spirit, with our divine creator. Prayer gifts us with the ability to be of service to God and live in union with all people and all things.

Discovery Thoughts

How do you choose to communicate with the divine creator?

....

What prayers have been answered in your life? How have those experiences changed you?

....

Affirmation: "My life is a prayer of thanksgiving. Prayer enlightens me."

....

Now add an affirmative thought to continue your flow of positive energy: "I . . ."

....

Community: A State of Unity

"I turn to the Presence of God at the center of my being, and it is here that I discover the nature of the Good which must and does reside in the back of all people and events."

—Ernest Holmes

Unity is wholeness beyond the self, one with all living things. It is a level of completeness that elevates us to a higher level of understanding, giving, and receiving.

As spiritual beings in human form we seek to live in equilibrium and in peace. This is intended for the greater good and the evolution of mankind. It may be difficult to embrace unity when we are aware of chaotic and devastating events in our world that we do not easily understand and that can seem insurmountable.

Community involves the people within your reach—who and what you interface with, relate to, and communicate with. Your reach may be your family and neighborhood, your place of work, and organizations you belong to. Geographically (which is a very human way to measure), it may include a very small or extensive area. Electronically, community interface may stretch to a vast number of people through internet connections and social media. However you define your community, whatever the depth of that relationship, know that it involves others, other spiritual beings in physical form, all of us living our lives to the best of our ability at any given time.

Forming relationships with others is our first experience with unity. Relationships reflect information back to us—who we are and where we are in our life processes. As we become more independent and self-aware our needs change, and thus the substance of our relationships change. Relationships build upon foundations. They are a continual pathway of exploration as we learn more about ourselves, our needs, and aspirations.

In the Soul Garden, we see relationships reflected in the growth of plants. Some are blooming, some have wilted, and some are tender seedlings. All relationships assist us in growth and should be honored. When we are in union with life, we recognize that even though we are each a unique individual we are all the same. We are divine beings of light and love.

"If you look deeply into the palm of your hand, you will see your parents and all generations of your ancestors. All of them are alive in this moment. Each is present in your body. You are the continuation of each of these people."

—Thich Nhat Hanh

Understand that in spiritual form we are all the same. On Earth, to live in unity, we are asked to share our gifts with others. Through our choices and experiences, we diversify and see ourselves as different. By the same token, by our choices and experiences, we can share in what is similar.

Begin with yourself. Begin with living in alignment with your higher self and making choices that promote your equilibrium, peace, and love. Ask Spirit to guide you always and bring your higher-self energy forward in all opportunities. We are evolving beings and capable of change.

We are meant to live in unity with all things, to share, to grow, to mature. Just as we do with the plants in our garden, we are meant to support and enhance each other's purpose and life. Community is a process of sharing while continuing to integrate and develop ourselves. In unity we embrace God in all his forms, and as Mother Teresa has so eloquently said, touch him in "his distressing disguise."

Discovery Thoughts

With increasing independence and self-awareness our needs change, and thus the substance of our relationships change. What do you value in a relationship?

....

Reflecting on your past relationships, who has influenced your growth the most?

....

How do you mentor others to support their growth and enlargement?

....

Affirmation: "I bloom in stages of completeness. My blossom supports the growth of others."

....

Now add an affirmative thought to continue your flow of positive energy: "I . . ."

....

In summary, dimensions of oneness include the seven states of being that are always present within us: serenity, alignment, flow, faith, love, prayer, and community. These dimensions describe the balance and alignment we are meant to live in and those we can create. We are like all others. By the grace of God, the benevolence of our creator, we are as we designed in the ethereal. No life is easy. Each of us has many challenges and obstacles, pain and suffering. We diversify through choice, and we are meant to learn and grow, and expand again.

"If the Angel deigns to come, it will be because you have convinced her, not by your tears, but by your humble resolve to be always beginning: to be a beginner."

—Rainer Maria Rilke, *Letters to a Young Poet*

LIFE IN THE GARDEN

From the Tree of Life, we create our Soul Garden. Energy, in the form of life force, creates seeds from thoughts, words, and actions that germinate to become seedlings. Each seedling vine and corresponding blossom are unique to an aspect of our life. We are always in the process of becoming. We are always growing upward in supplication, guided by light.

You have the ability to observe and reflect on your life processes and accumulated plants and blossoms as you walk among them, appreciating your gifts and accomplishments. You become aware of life changes and choices that altered your direction. You become aware of further growth and authenticity that guided you back into balance and alignment. It is all within your capability. Know that your garden is a place of discovery and wisdom.

Let's go to your Soul Garden for a while. Bring your mind to a place of calm. Relax with slow breaths and gradually envision your life in the garden as a perpetual place of beauty and growth. A haven, a heaven, and a sanctuary. You can go there anytime you want.

You are one with nature and one with all living things. As a being of light and love you generate energy in producing your garden. Think of yourself as a germinator, an initiator of all things beautiful as all the garden growth appears before you.

You are filled with gratitude. It overwhelms you with warmth circulating through your body to your heart. Now you understand the flow of gratitude. Gratitude is your heart speaking to you in kind.

"I am filled with gratitude for my life," you whisper with every breath.

It resonates. It reverberates within you.

And now you see how the divine creator sees you.

You are a beautiful divine child. You are always growing and always becoming *more*.

"I am filled with gratitude for my life," you whisper again as it becomes your mantra.

Gratitude creates grace.

Pope Francis told us that grace "is the amount of light in our souls, not knowledge nor reason." Grace is the light that blesses us and all our thoughts, words, and actions.

Grace is the light of God.

The garden is a safe place of discovery and wisdom. Envision your garden with your Tree of Life in the center. The Tree of Life is also the central place of mind, body, and spirit that aligns and grounds you. Whenever you feel out of balance, this is where you belong: sitting with your back against the tree, one with all there is.

The energy from your every thought, word, and action creates the seeds of your life, what you wish to plant. The seeds take root and begin their process of growth. Like all things, it is a developmental process. Roots give rise to seedlings and seedlings generate stems and leaves and then continue to gift us with blossoms. This is the life cycle of our seeds.

Changes and choices we make in our life may alter the growth of our seeds and the growth of all living things in the garden.

The Helix of Growth: The Garden Matrix

"Then I began to realize that I had to take another step in my evolution and growth."

—Eileen Caddy

The helix of growth is an internal support to the stems of our plants. It represents the actionizing component of our development and maturation, meaning that when the supporting structures of the helix (development, experience, and expansion) are in place, they promote forward progress. Within the stem of our plants, the helix of growth curls like DNA strands and continues to twist in repeated steps of advancement. You may assess this forward progress as having negative or positive results. The helix is required to sustain our growth.

Growth is a process that requires us to develop physically, mindfully, emotionally, and spiritually. Each progression of the helix has a higher function than the previous, a higher level of understanding and ability. These are small steps with ascending levels. For instance, I can have the developmental ability to walk. From there, I experience crossing the street while holding someone's hand. Because that was successful, I have gained the confidence to expand myself and independently cross the street.

Development, Experience, and Expansion

Development

With each stage of development, we increase abilities. These can be physical, mental, emotional, or spiritual. Each stage allows us to increase our skills, insight, and competence. Developmental growth increases confidence and the will to strive to be and do *more*.

Experience

All experiences are learnings. They are meant to help us on our life journey. We experience consciously or subconsciously, actively or passively. In the process of experiencing, we choose next actions and establish leaves of progression displayed along the flower stems, the outcomes of our learnings. We may not understand these learnings at the time. If we continue to ask, "Why? Why did this happen?" we are seeking answers to satisfy judgmental thoughts and gain control over future instances. Some things we may never understand. In those situations, we are not meant to. Remember that experiences are designed *for* us, not as something happening *to* us.

We are asked to trust.

We consciously make choices to move from where we are to a different position. Choices create change. You may make a choice believing you will move ahead and step forward or perhaps step to the side. We make hundreds of choices every day, many of which are automatic or made unconsciously.

Think about your drive to work. You know the way, and every time you turn right or left you are *following* the way, not consciously *choosing* the way. But if there is a detour you must shift your thinking into conscious choices (perhaps with the help of GPS!).

The choices we make influence our growth, wellness, and consciousness as we interpret and embody their outcomes. Our ability to make choices corresponds to our capabilities, knowledge, independence, needs, and aspirations. These change over time as we increasingly understand ourselves and our purpose in life. Ultimately, it is not what we choose that matters. Our power to influence future outcomes lies in our reasons for making a certain choice. When our choices are aligned with authenticity and higher self, they are blessed.

Through our growth, we gain abilities, insight, wisdom, confidence, and trust in ourselves and the law of divine order and timing. We can increase our trust in universal design and know we are part of a greater plan.

Expansion

Expansion is the result of the embodiment of learnings. With expansion we grow in wisdom, understanding, intuition, and acceptance. Expansion allows us to view and approach the world with increased awareness, opening ourselves more fully to the flow of divine love and light. Expansion is the progressive growth of trust.

"When we come to an edge we come to a frontier that tells us that we are now about to become more than we have been before."

—William Irwin Thompson

Leaves of progression mark the incorporation of learning that occurs at each plateau of the helix. To begin growth, we set an intention by affirmation, desire, or prayer.

The stem of the plant continues to develop into a bud and will yield a blossom when the plant has ripened to its fullest state of learning. Blossoms may occur singularly or in groups. They may be partially or fully open. Blossoms indicate that an attribute toward wholeness has achieved a level of expansion.

Life in the Soul Garden is one of growth. Growth occurs with development, experience, and expansion. These are influenced by our choices and free will.

Discovery Thoughts

Using the helix of growth as a model, what process aspect of your development, experience, and expansion are you currently in?

....

What do you feel are the next steps in evolving your life?

....

Growth occurs from the perception of positive and negative experiences. How have experiences influenced your choices?

....

Affirmation: "I grow with the freedom of my choices. My life continuously creates through expansion."

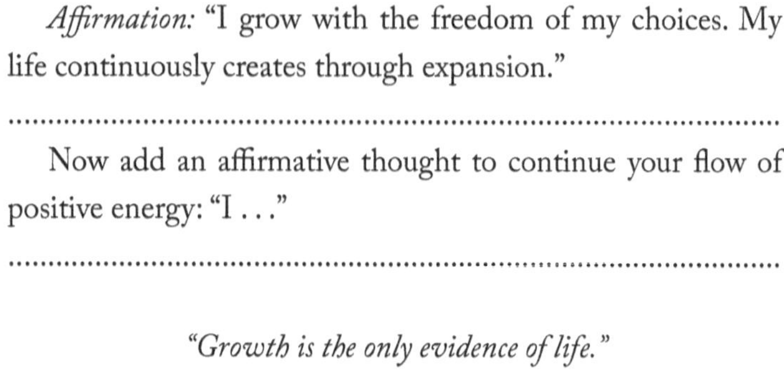

Now add an affirmative thought to continue your flow of positive energy: "I . . ."

"*Growth is the only evidence of life.*"

—John Henry Newman

Maturity

"*Maybe being oneself is an acquired taste.*"

—Patricia Hampl

Human development is an innate process of evolution and maturation that crosses all dimensions of life: ethereal, mind, body, spirit, and transition. These processes uniquely differentiate each of us from all other people, as individual beings of light in human form.

Maturity is a subjective opinion of our behavior, thoughts, and beliefs. Typically, as we mature, we age, gain new skills, knowledge, insight, and capabilities. Our stages of development proceed in sequential patterns and include qualitative and quantitative changes in verbal acuity, cognitive aptitude, behavior, dexterity, coordination, processing, and independence. Each of these is characterized by specific milestones that correlate with our abilities, needs, intentions, and goals. We choose to be more of a person that we like and admire. We hopefully become more of the type of person we are meant to be.

Each of us grows at our own pace and attains specific levels of functioning when we are physically, mentally, and emotionally ready. Our experiences and proficiency can motivate us to move forward, gaining confidence and independence. The world outside ourselves has many factors that influence our thought processes and decisions. Rules, governmental laws, family and friends, commitments, circumstances, and careers contain some level of power to direct us. Depending upon our relationship with those factors, we may be swayed to a higher or lesser degree of growth.

Likewise, the world inside of us is very powerful. The ego mind creates stories in our mind that depict us as the main character, always in search of control and power. We form feelings, opinions, and judgments that we may emotionally attach to. The ability to interpret information increases as the ability of the mind grows multidimensionally. Interpretation can be based on experiences, personal preferences, learnings, opinions, and things imagined or created. Underlying our reasoning is an expanding concept of truth—in ourselves, others, and the world at any given moment in time. Interpretation is situational, meaning that it relies on what we can grasp with the resources we currently have. Interpretation adds certainty to our beliefs.

Beyond this, our spiritual connection to heart, to higher self, frees us to be objective and loving. The spirit of love is our most powerful and far-reaching influence.

Emergency departments are open all day and night to receive all kinds of patients, all ages, and with all kinds of problems. When I began to have children of my own, I found it emotionally harder to work in emergency departments and receive young patients who were severely injured or compromised. They came back to me in my dreams. I prayed for them and blessed them. I will never forget one boy, about ten years old, who had been in a car accident. The ambulance brought him in on a backboard with a cervical neck collar on to keep him immobile. It was obvious he had a head injury. His father had died in the accident.

His mother arrived in a whirlwind, desperate, expressing guilt for not having been in the car. I took her to the boy's room, moved a chair close to the stretcher, and created a way for her to touch her son. She was too afraid to cry. The physician told her the critical results of the tests and that he was making calls for her son to transfer to Boston where he could receive neurological care that we didn't have. She only nodded. It was all arranged quickly. The ambulance came and they loaded him into the back. They allowed his mother to ride in the front of the truck with them as she had no car or other way to get there.

Sirens blaring, lights flashing, they were gone into the night. Some staff had started to clean the room, but I took the backboard into the utility room to wash it. It was covered in the boy's blood and some fragments of skin and tissue. I stayed there for quite a while, and they let me. I cried the tears his mother couldn't. I prayed for his safety and his life. I prayed for benevolence and grace. I prayed for his mother, that she would know again the love they shared. He came to me in my dreams.

A few days later we called the unit where the boy had been admitted to get an update. We knew his prognosis was very poor and indeed they told us he had passed away. But they wanted us to know that before he died, they helped his mother crawl into bed beside him, to cradle him, and hold him once more. He died in her arms that night.

I know the grace of God.

*"Out of every crisis comes the chance to be reborn,
to reconceive ourselves as individuals, to choose the kind of change that
will help us to grow and to fulfill ourselves more completely."*

—Nena O'Neill

All our choices contribute to revealing our personality and individuality. In that way we are visible to others. This may create attraction or rejection, or neutral energy flow. Staying true to who you are rather than who you think you should be is an important step in gaining levels of maturity.

If we make our choices from a place of integrity and alignment, we progressively gain abilities to make better choices for ourselves as we mature. Remember that at any given point in time we can only utilize the information and perspective we currently have to make choices. Interpretation is situational. This is a great thing to remember about other people's choices as well.

Work situations are always interesting. While everyone may try to leave their "home life" at home, home life invariably sneaks in at times. I learned as a manager that when someone is having an "off day," as we called it, meaning they are not communicating well or working well as a team member, there is always more to the story. The unit you work in, the staff you work with, is your second family. They support you and circle around you in all times of need. These are the times when we might make assumptions and conclude that someone is underperforming or uncaring. But then we hear about someone finding a lump in their breast, the loss of a spouse's job, their child who's been suspended from school, or the decision to divorce. There is no distinction between the stresses of life outside of the hospital and the challenges within. The only separation is our judgments and criticism.

The journey of maturity includes the development and expansion of our belief system and exploring the purpose of our existence, our life's purpose. Everything is in constant evolution by design, and change is an integral part of that process. Questions arise as well as conflicts. We desire to know more and to make our own choices, but the rules, responsibilities, and expectations engrained in us in childhood are remnants of security blankets we hold on to as our values and morals. It is sometimes easier to hang on than to deal with mental conflict.

As a child in the 1950s and '60s, I was greatly influenced by my parents and religious doctrine. My parents promoted and rewarded obedience, and I transferred that to include compliance with their beliefs. Clearly the arguments over the dinner table were less loud with compliance. The church's views on sexual relationships and women's rights brought choices forward for me to consider in my life. I was not conflicted as much as I was excited about these otherwise unheard-of opportunities. In the seventies, everyone was speaking out and demanding to be heard! For the first time I felt that I was thinking for myself. Promoted by the environment, experiences, and my evolving lifestyle, I adopted new behaviors and viewpoints. Still, I had not yet learned the fine art of soul searching. I married in my senior year of college. I was no longer going to be the "unpredictable" author—I could be the predictable wife playing an expected role. Fast-forward, that never happened. I am not a good actress.

Understand that your growth is not dependent on you knowing *why* things have happened or changed, but to accept what you can, knowing circumstances will change again over time. As they change life gives us a new view. Trust. Growth relies on openness and acceptance, and belief in the evolution of ourselves and humanity for the greatest good of all.

The affirmation that follows is a direct connection to being able to see anew from a higher level: "I am alive in the truth of the present. I embrace growth through change."

Discovery Thoughts

Thoughts are influenced by many experiences and beliefs. What influences your thinking?

....

How do perceptions influence your choices?

....

Affirmation: "I am alive in the truth of the present. I embrace growth through change."

....

Now add an affirmative thought to continue your flow of positive energy: "I . . ."

....

Living in Spiritual Grace

"Gardening is an instrument of grace."

—May Sarton

A sanctuary is a place of repose and refuge, a place of peace. In the physical world it can be associated with the holiest part of a temple or church, a sacred space. Likewise, the sanctuary of your soul brings you closest to your spirit, the higher power that lives within you.

Your spiritual relationship is one of freedom—to be your authentic self, to create all you desire, to love without limits, and to be one in unity with all.

Remember that you are a steward for your garden and your life on Earth. Our garden exists in living gratitude and blesses us. In your Soul Garden life appears as unimaginable beauty. Everything you have ever needed or desired exists along your soul's pathway. Its magnificence glows from the splendor of blooms to the most delicate petal flushed with dew. You are surrounded in a world of flourishing life, the seeds of your lifetimes. From the Tree of Life, paths weave through memories, experiences, and emotions. You may wander as you choose, observing and contemplating the years that have produced them, the path you are now walking, and the future you aspire to.

"When the soul wishes to experience something, she throws an image of the experience out before her and enters into her own image."

—Meister Eckhart

Your Soul Garden is a place of multidimensional capability, a quantum field where all there can be, and all that is, is as it was meant to be. You are meant to create abundance for yourself and others, in nature and within the earthly plane.

Jill Jackson-Miller wrote the song "Let There Be Peace on Earth," which speaks to higher self-understanding. The peace inside us and that which we project out into the world is living in alignment with spiritual grace.

Using the energy within you, proportional in magnitude to the vibrational frequency it represents, you continue to create your life through your thoughts, words, and actions. You are meant to create a life for yourself and all others through your positive energy and authenticity. The higher the frequency your energy represents, the more love you project into the world. The higher your frequency, the more you are apt to live in balance and alignment with spiritual goodness, which flows to you.

You are part of a collective consciousness that is pure energy. You are the essence of life on Earth. What do you want to create?

What we dwell on and focus on is what we give and receive, and what we plant.

The seeds of your desires need nourishment to grow. What you pay attention to will grow. You are the nurturer. It is important to have a clear intention and focus—not just for yourself, but for all others with what you project.

Every moment in your life is life breathing and flowing into you. Say thank you for every moment, for each wave of divine energy as it pulsates through you. Bless it.

Bless everything you perceive to be an obstacle for its divine purpose, which is to teach you through experience. Learning is a steppingstone that elevates us to higher thinking.

How do you ask for the blessing of grace upon yourself?

Ask for blessings upon your choices, upon all you do and are, and all you want to be.

How do you bestow grace upon others?

Bless them at all times, whatever they do, whoever they are. Your blessing will promote goodness within their physical being and activate motion.

Discovery Thoughts

Imagine you are standing in your Soul Garden. How do you feel spiritually connected?

....

The high frequency of our vibrational energy gives us multi-dimensional capabilities. Using this energy source, what would you create?

....

Affirmation: "I am a sacred instrument of spiritual energy. I create love and abundance."

....

Now add an affirmative thought to continue your flow of positive energy: "I . . ."

....

Chapter 6

Burgeoning Life

"And the day came when the risk to remain tight in a bud was more painful than the risk it took to blossom."

—attributed to Anaïs Nin

Now come to your Soul Garden, the garden you have created from your thoughts, words, and actions. You are the origin as well as the creator. You are your Tree of Life connecting your mind, body, and spirit to you and all things beyond you. A part of you is reflected in the beauty and growth of each plant. The many attributes and colors differentiate you from others. This is your life story.

This chapter aligns you with what you can create and reminds you of what you have created. It asks you to embrace your garden life and discover how it speaks to you.

All growth is a process of expansion. In our divinely planned world, the processes of growth are duplicated within the same plant species. Think about the factors needed to become a flower in bloom. Consider the seed in its natural form. To begin germination, a seed must have a support place that initiates and triggers its life to begin anew. It may be blown in the wind or carried by birds. It may land in dirt or water or a very unfertile space like the roof of a building. The chances of even beginning germination are complicated at best. We are blessed to plant a seed, either consciously or subconsciously, that germinates.

The shell of the seed, its protection, must be exposed to earth, water, air, and the energy of the sun. The seed shell begins to soften, split, and slowly sprout. Shedding protective layers, a shoot expands upward toward the sun and below to root to secure itself. As roots grow, they anchor into the ground, shedding their seed covering and providing a channel for energy from the plant to ground back into the earth. A sprout rises from the seed seeking light. The seed is new life, expanding above and below.

Sprouts gain strength and the capacity to become seedlings, then grow as shoots with stems and leaves that can be identified as specific types of plants through their unique characteristics. Stems grow longer and stronger and advance in the three-process helix of growth as we do: development, experience, and expansion.

"The growth of understanding follows an ascending spiral rather than a straight line."

—Joanna Field

Based on what kind of plant it is, there are external and internal factors that determine and influence what it will produce. If the plant is to bloom, a bud will form at the tip of the seedling wrapped in protective leaf coverings. The bud is encased to ensure it will have optimum time to develop and be protected. The emerging bud is one of the most vulnerable states in plant life. If it opens, it is exposed, and its inner beauty becomes visible. If it does not, there will not be any new seed growth. In many ways it will be the end of its life cycle.

Progressive stages of development and the warmth of light signal a time for the bud to reveal itself. In circular succession, protective leaves peel back and tender petals begin to separate from the hull. With every advancement, more of the bloom becomes fully visible. It is the next phase in the life of the plant, and an expression of courage. In this brief time of opening, its beauty and fragrance permeate the air. The bloom exposes itself to nature—bees, butterflies, and birds—to fulfill its purpose of nourishing the garden.

Blossoming is a state of growth that parallels our own stages of maturity as we open to our authenticity—the person we are and the person we are becoming. Consider our humanness in its natural form in relation to the seed. Our support place is the womb. Our fertilized egg is the seed shell opening and growing outward: head, arms, and legs. If fully planted, the egg can develop further and grow the details of eyes and nose, fingers and toes. Our first blossoming is our birth, one of the most vulnerable states of our existence.

In our youngest years we continue to gain strength, definition, and character traits unique to ourselves. We continue to rely on our family unit for nourishment and support. We can begin to show our personality, preferences, and accomplishments like the plant showing its leaves and colors. Early growth, experiences, and expansions generally relate to our environment, our family unit, and people and places we interfaced with.

In the Soul Garden, blossoms that reach full expansion and exposure have reached a state of enlightenment. The flower willingly shares its beauty and its attributes for all others to enjoy. As a human being in physical form, we choose what to reveal and share. Blossoming is our time of uncovering ourselves, for us and others to truly see.

Seedlings

"Once you are real you can't become unreal again. It lasts for always."

—Margery Williams, *The Velveteen Rabbit*

We choose the seeds we plant. Seedlings are a magnificent display of hope, of life anew. As the seedling grows it makes itself more visible, understanding that all is finely orchestrated in divine order and timing. The stem thickens and lengthens while leaves of progression emerge from the stem at predictable intervals. The stem is an indication of the overall health of the plant while the leaves are an outward sign of achievements.

Physical abilities, knowledge, mindfulness, comprehension, beliefs, self-worth, confidence, consciousness, independence, and emotional maturity are examples of outcomes we can experience and display. Growth activates consciousness and increases our capacity to understand ourselves, our needs, and our choices.

A plant has sensing capabilities that help it to thrive. It senses the best orientation to gain sun exposure and leans its stem to follow that track. Leaf growth assists with water absorption and protection. Roots divide and multiply to add stability and to grow beyond barriers, such as rocks, that are in the soil. Roots can also change direction of growth to optimize their functions, such as to gain more exposure to light or find more fertile soil.

For humans, actionizing stem phases of growth represent the ways we incorporate higher functions and capabilities into our life. This usually occurs in an expected order of development. With this growth we expand our abilities and their purposes. Often our purpose is to utilize these abilities and master them to their fullest extent using the many aspects of our mind, body, and spirit to achieve a goal.

There are nine types of seedling growth or stem phases. Each phase is an aspect of functionality and associated subcategories that further define its purpose.

As you read through the different aspects of functionality, what comes to mind for you? Do specific terms have a deeper meaning and relevance in your life? Consider how you incorporate these traits into your growth.

Can you describe how you were further impacted or changed by them? You are the stem leaning to track the sun and the roots circumventing rocks in your path. What other descriptive words come to mind?

Consider what you have achieved and embodied into your life processes to experience more growth as you reseed and replant. Positive life skills facilitate optimum growth and well-being.

"We are the flow; we are the ebb. We are the weavers; we are the web."

—Shekhinah Mountainwater

States of Seedling Growth (Aspects of Functionality)

Sensing

Our abilities to interpret when we sense are stimulated to know more or understand better. We often develop an associated reaction when we sense. When we are exposed again, that same reaction or emotion may surface. For example, with the smell of roses, I immediately visualize my father who doted on his rose garden in the backyard and faithfully brought my mother a rose each morning with her coffee. A very tender remembrance.

* *Hearing* incorporates sounds. Sounds create thoughts, images, and reactions like fear or relaxation.

* *Touch* creates feelings. We comprehend softness, roughness, heat, and cold. We differentiate them by sensing those that are pleasant and those that are uncomfortable.

* *Seeing* displays the functionality of our eyes, and on a deeper level the ability of our mind to sense reality and truth.

* *Tasting* awakens tastebuds, saliva, and responses to food and drink that include satisfaction and security.

* *Olfaction*, our sense of smell, is a message system alerting us to our surroundings. Smells may be comforting, inviting, pleasant, toxic, or acrid.

Developing: Abilities Often Associated with Age

* Emerging: Becoming visible
* Growing: Increasing, enlarging
* Progressing: Advancing
* Becoming: Forming
* Standing: Being upright, balanced
* Maturing: Coming of age, understanding with broader perspective
* Expanding: Becoming multidimensional
* Enlightening: Illuminating
* Transitioning: Changing multi-levels

Communicating: Forms of Expression and Conveyance

* Speaking: Using voice, tone, loudness
* Asking: Questioning, inquiring
* Expressing: Articulating, detailing
* Requesting: Asking for desires and needs
* Describing: Telling
* Listening: Receiving
* Conversing: Sharing mutually
* Elaborating: Detailing
* Negotiating: Bargaining
* Storytelling: Creating
* Vibrating: Communicating energy

Living: Aspects of Expansion

- ❋ Being: Living, allowing
- ❋ Belonging: Feeling attachment
- ❋ Experiencing: Having exposure to
- ❋ Embracing: Incorporating
- ❋ Releasing: Letting go
- ❋ Freeing: Liberating
- ❋ Rejoicing: Celebrating
- ❋ Pursuing: Following
- ❋ Initiating: Starting
- ❋ Actionizing: Triggering
- ❋ Strengthening: Making stronger, tempering, fortifying
- ❋ Receiving: Obtaining
- ❋ Motivating: Inspiring
- ❋ Energizing: Invigorating
- ❋ Relating: Associating with
- ❋ Exploring: Investigating
- ❋ Discovering: Bringing forth awareness

Thinking: Translation Within the Mind

- ❋ Feeling: Absorbing
- ❋ Interpreting: Deciphering
- ❋ Contemplating: Considering
- ❋ Questioning: Clarifying
- ❋ Learning: Grasping, understanding
- ❋ Knowing: Being conscious of
- ❋ Processing: Using methodology

- Assessing: Analyzing
- Evaluating: Appraising
- Organizing: Sorting
- Perceiving: Recognizing
- Filtering: Refining
- Choosing: Selecting

Creating: Influencing Outward

- Hoping: Anticipating
- Desiring: Yearning
- Dreaming: Wishing
- Envisioning: Imagining
- Designing: Outlining
- Projecting: Sending out
- Manifesting: Building from thought
- Illuminating: Revealing
- Mirroring: Reflecting
- Germinating: Emerging

Being of Service: Beyond Self

- Caring: Being kindhearted
- Helping: Accommodating
- Aiding: Assisting
- Giving: Acting charitably
- Sharing: Portioning
- Nurturing: Tending
- Mentoring: Guiding

* Inspiring: Motivating
* Supporting: Encouraging
* Loving: Being devoted to

Praying: One with Spirit

* Meditating: Contemplating
* Thanking: Expressing gratitude
* Forgiving: Excusing, releasing
* Accepting: Agreeing to
* Allowing: Opening, permitting
* Believing: Trusting
* Communing: Being as one
* Blessing: Invoking

Integrating: Aligning Energetically

* Absorbing: Incorporating
* Connecting: Joining
* Coordinating: Synchronizing
* Balancing: Stabilizing
* Surrendering: Yielding
* Inner child: Being one with physical being
* Higher self: Being one with spiritual self
* Assimilating: Making sense of
* Transcending: Going beyond
* Ascending: Rising above
* Intuiting: Using instinct

*"It's when we're given choice that we sit with the gods
and design ourselves."*

—Dorothy Gilman

Seedlings are the actionizing elements of our life that we have chosen to cultivate. Each assists us in continuing growth processes to live more fully and further develop our uniqueness as divine beings of light and love.

Discovery Thoughts

Choose a seedling growth category and describe how you have grown and matured in this area of your life.

....

The helix of growth progresses by development, experience, and expansion. In reflecting on your life, what expansive learning was pivotal in leading you to the present?

....

Leaves of progression are the outcomes of your experiences. What outcomes do you wish to manifest from your experiences?

....

Affirmation: "My life offers me unlimited experiences and manifested outcomes. Joy surrounds me!"

....

Now add an affirmative thought to continue your flow of positive energy: "I . . ."

....

"I like to think of thoughts as living blossoms borne by the human tree."

—James Douglas

Blossoms

"Every flower is a soul blossoming in nature."

—Gérard de Nerval

With the subject of blossoms, we move into the phase of harvesting and the beautiful yield of our plants and life choices—creations from the life we live. Blossoms in the Soul Garden are the summation of your thoughts, words, and actions throughout your lifetime and all your lifetimes. We are beings of divine light cultivating our lives and sharing the blossoms that come forth for us and others to appreciate.

The green outer petal leaves cover and protect the bud in its last phase of opening. This is the time when buds are most vulnerable to predators. Insects, caterpillars, deer, and woodchucks all seek the tender, sweet taste of buds.

Think of times in your life when you have been ready to bloom. You may have anxiety and doubt about showing yourself in such an exposed way. You may be targeted by people who want you to fail and to be less than who you are. You know, however, that it is time to peel back your outer layers and display your heart and the gifts you are blessed with. These are the gifts you are meant to share.

Inside the outer covering of the blossom, the protective petals, the petals of assimilation, begin to unfold. They may be one color or multiple colors, one shade or variations from light to dark. What is assimilation? It is a process of integration. As the petals unfold, the intricate aspects of yourself are being revealed.

As spiritual beings in physical form, we are also guided by dynamic forces. Light and darkness are both stimulating and balancing as evidenced by the seasons of the year. We could not grow or survive without this dichotomy: time to work and time to rest.

When a flower blooms, unfolding its petals to reveal its heart, it is at the highest level of its life cycle. Each petal is a symbol of our journey, each color a symbol of spiritual energy that encourages, promotes, and gives sustenance to garden life.

During blooming, immature seeds are produced in the blossom and released with the purpose of regeneration, the act of renewal. Healthy plants will display resistance to disease and resilience in the face of inclement weather.

The process of blooming occurs in three stages as the plant reaches maturity. For us, these stages are intention, manifestation, and realization.

The bud represents intention, the desire to become a flower in bloom. Intention is an act of the mind. With intention, you are creating thoughts of what you desire to become.

The petals represent the products of manifestation. Manifestation is visualizing, believing, and allowing thoughts to come forward in a materialized form.

The blossom represents the realization of discovery, maturity, or truth. It is the discovery of your own truth and authenticity. As the bud blooms, you attain a higher level of maturity and understanding of your life.

Each blossom creates seeds that seek to perpetuate the goodness and kindness you have brought into the world or wanted to bring into the world. They seek to support future growth, promote a higher level of attainment, and be of service for the higher good.

Plants usually have more than one bloom and may continue to bloom throughout a season. This prolific disbursement of future growth at one time or multiple times represents what was manifested at any given time.

Spiritual energy in the form of messages and guidance encourages us to be more of what we can be so we can continue to expand. Experiences in prayer, meditation, and connection with angels clarify and enhance our thinking. These connections are available to all of us to utilize. The only limitations are those that we place upon ourselves.

The further unfolding of petals reveals the heart of the blossom. The heart is the innermost place of source energy, vulnerability, and truth.

Think about the association of vulnerability and truth. When you are your most authentic self, do you feel exposed or energized by your freedom?

"Bloom where you're planted."

—Mary Engelbreit

Attributes of Blossoms

There are six types of attributes associated with blossoms and the goals we attain in life. As you walk your path, varying attributes will emerge based on the situation and the experience. These are self-assessment attributes based on how you perceive your experiences and expansion. Thinking about cultivating these blossoms in our life is how we learn and gain confidence.

As you review these blossoms, these attributes, and their corresponding petals of assimilation, think about how they are meaningful to your life.

Truth is your own truth, not living up to someone else's expectations and definitions. Truth and sincerity go hand in hand in establishing a guidepost for our communications and behaviors.

* Accuracy
* Correctness
* Validity
* Factuality

* Integrity
* Wholeness
* Sincerity
* Authenticity
* Honesty
* Candor
* Principle
* Certainty
* Openness
* Forthrightness

Love is the intimacy we feel with ourselves (self-love) and the benevolence we exhibit in our relationships with people and all living things.

* Attachment
* Security
* Affection
* Belonging
* Joy
* Benevolence
* Embrace and release
* Compassion
* Sympathy
* Self-esteem
* Love of self
* Devotion
* Agape
* Adoration

* Gratitude
* Kindness
* Charity
* Giving
* Philanthropy
* Altruism

Faith is a state of belief and trust we embody when connecting mentally (through the mind) and/or spiritually (through the heart) with a concept, theory, or principle. Our degree of faith may be influenced by other people and groups or institutions. Our blossoms allow us to see what is truly our own and how they have connected along the stem of our growth with other attributes.

* Belief
* Ideology
* Interpretation
* Opinion
* Sentiment
* Reliance
* Obedience
* Commitment
* Dedication
* Loyalty
* Conviction
* Assurance
* Optimism
* Confidence
* Credence

Spirituality is a noun that describes the sacred and ethereal embodiment of higher-self concepts. Your spiritual life and awareness are in a constant state of discovery and growth.

* Karma
* Chakras
* Higher calling
* Adoration
* Inspiration
* Higher self
* "I AM"
* Soul purpose
* Life path
* One as whole
* One with Spirit

Intuition, the sixth sense, enhances all our other senses (hearing, sight, smell, touch, taste) to a higher level of perception and understanding. Intuition gives rise to knowing without physical proof. It utilizes our degree of allowing intangible things to come forward to the mind and then act on them.

* Inherent
* Innate
* Instinct
* Visceral
* Sensitivity
* Perception
* Insight
* Premonition
* Vibration

* Déjà vu
* Clairvoyance
* Visionary
* Third eye

Surrender is the degree of openness we assume as situations and circumstances come into our lives. It is not an abdication of our free will or mindfulness. True surrender is trust and faith in allowing the spiritual self to guide and direct us.

* Allowing
* Openness
* Sacrifice
* Capitulation
* Acceptance
* Service
* Freedom
* Conceding
* Relenting
* Submission
* Acquiescence
* Relinquishing
* Yielding

"God is in the details."

—Ludwig Mies van der Rohe

Blossoms are the product of our purposeful intention, manifestation, and realization. They complete stages of growth cycles and provide a visual representation of our creation and journey. Blossoms bring beauty and richness to the garden, increase our understanding of individualization, and, with kindness and vulnerability, seek to support other life.

Discovery Thoughts

Choose one of the six types of blossoms (attributes) in which you have experienced blooming. Describe that growth and what it represented to you.

....

Affirmation: "I am beautiful. My life blooms with my creativity."

....

Now add an affirmative thought to continue your flow of positive energy: "I . . ."

....

Sun and Shade Plants

"I have a little shadow that goes in and out with me, And what can be the use of him is more than I can see."

—Robert Louis Stevenson, "My Shadow"

We are part light and part shade. Our shadow follows us wherever we go. It is as much a part of us as our physical being, the things we can touch and feel. It is interesting that our shadow is visible when pictures are taken. Altered by light, it has form, dimensions, and character.

All plantings and plants have purpose and usefulness. Perhaps they are not as we originally intended or in the degree that they live up to our expectations, but in time we can more objectively view them as a contribution to our development. And in our garden, as in our lives, we need balance. What we perceive as opposites assist us in gaining equilibrium and balance in our lives. Like night and day, both sun and shade plants are needed to complete the natural order of things.

Thriving in the shade is not a negative trait. Plants show us a way forward even in difficult circumstances. They can adjust to changing conditions and environments. A shade plant can remain in the shade while always being drawn to the light. Roots will always gravitate to the light, acquiring additional energy to use for the highest good and to send nourishing energy back to the earth. We are also drawn to the light and the positivity in the world, guided by our inner voice and the conviction of our values and beliefs.

Your garden assists you in finding your voice and living authentically. It increases your awareness of the life you have experienced, your choices and outcomes. We need to give our plants recognition for the purposes they have brought forward. Both light and dark enhance our individualization.

"Flowers grow out of dark moments."

—Corita Kent

How do shade plants appear in the garden? They do grow in darker places and therefore are symbols of strength and courage. They may appear hidden or shy as they sit beneath taller and bushier vegetation that provides shelter for them.

Shade plants usually have more intricate and detailed leaf structures than sun plants and may grow extensive vines. Although not as colorful or flamboyant as their cousins, they display unique qualities specific to their species.

The predominant color of shade plants is green—the color associated with photosynthesis (energy conversion), fertility, and healing.

Green in all its shades evokes thoughts of nature, growth, renewal, and abundance.

Shade plants offer a different perspective and allow us to look at life with more discrimination. Experiences we consider part of our shadow side that contain negativity, anger, and jealousy, for instance, ultimately promote learning and the establishment of new roots. When we evaluate what is best for our growth, we give plants recognition for the purpose they've had in increasing our awareness to make changes. Through the growth of our shadow plants, we are better able to understand the life processes of others with compassion and empathy.

Things we see in a shadow or negative light reflect how we view and judge others and ourselves. Dr. Wayne Dyer expresses this beautifully when he tells us to "remember the truth I've written about many times: You do not attract what you want; You attract what you are." The shadow side assists you in finding your voice and living authentically.

Love your shadow unconditionally. Love yourself fully for who you truly are. In striving for perfection, we may reject unique aspects of ourselves. When you love and accept your shadow side, you can reclaim your gifts to be one with all. Acknowledge what these plants have brought forward in your life and how they promote your growth and wellness.

Discovery Thoughts

What characteristics do you see in your shade plants? How do you incorporate them into the garden?

....

Affirmation: "I love myself fully and unconditionally. I give myself divine love."

....

Now add an affirmative thought to continue your flow of positive energy: "I . . ."

....

CHAPTER 7

THE SPIRITUAL GARDENER

—Barbara Damrosch

We all create Soul Gardens, but we do not all become spiritual gardeners. To become a spiritual gardener is a conscious choice we make as we live our life and navigate our pathways. There are no prerequisites to being a spiritual gardener. By birth, as a spiritual being in physical form, the role of gardener is part of our lineage and heritage. It is a gift that is before all of us, for us to participate in and, therefore, to be able to know more of our true selves.

Age varies, but for many there is an increased spiritual enlightenment between adolescence and adulthood that allows mindful thoughts to find their connection to heart and higher self. That connection is necessary to enter the garden. The role of a spiritual gardener requires some routine work, awareness, and attention. Without this effort, the garden itself will continue to produce and grow as it desires, exercising its free will in any direction. The longer the Soul Garden is unattended, the more complicated it can be to identify a plant from weeds and the confusing underbrush—in other words, meaningless additions.

The quote from Barbara Damrosch brings attention to the basic needs of plants: "Good gardening is very simple, really. You just have to learn to think like a plant." To me, this asks us to simplify what we feel is necessary both in the garden and in our lives. Core needs for plants and for humans are oxygen, light, water, and nutrients.

With a Soul Garden in mind, we can start to review what we have planted. We can reflect on how a seed was created, why a plant has grown, and how the plant benefits the garden overall. Has this plant become a weed over time?

Growth is a natural order of life. If we look to nature as an example, as long as its minimal basic needs are met, growth will still occur even when nothing is done to promote it. Nature seeks to thrive and rebalance on its own.

Interestingly, the seven basic needs of plants and humans, which further benefit life and growth, are also the same:

* **Earth:** To root ourselves in solid ground and connect with the energy of Mother Earth.

* **Water:** To hydrate us and assist in transportation of nutrients throughout our physical being. Water is also a conductor of vibrational energy, such as sound waves.

* **Sunlight:** To promote many necessary processes, including photosynthesis in plants and the absorption of vitamin D in humans. It keeps us warm and enhances our ability to see.

* **Protection:** To keep us safe from predators, inclement weather, and disease.

* **Roots:** To provide balance and stability.

* **Food/Nutrients:** To ingest or be absorbed to promote health and wellness.

* **Space:** To enlarge without constraints or limitations, to grow to our fullest potential, to experience freedom.

Divine order and divine timing allow us to know that all growth occurs as planned. All cells in our body are structured to replicate either by division or multiplication. Once an egg is fertilized, it begins these processes. Once a seed lands in a place suitable for growth, it begins to germinate.

Seasons

"There is no season such delight can bring as summer,
autumn, winter, and spring."

—William Browne

Divine order and divine timing are also part of the annual repetition of the seasons. A season can be a phase of life or growth. Every season has a primary purpose and responsibility in the garden, and each season represents time to be used in a constructive way. They are cyclic in their sequences that allow natural flow into the next progression of life. Each season promotes necessary actions to reset and begin again. We parallel the seasons of the year in our processes of growth as they ask us to rest, rebirth, expand, and reap. Our plants and our selves show us that we are more alike than different.

Using the gifts of the seasons opens us to receive their maximum benefits.

Winter is a time of rest. Our plants sleep in the cold under the silent earth. In this dormant period that seems like a pause in time, we rest to clear our minds, heal our bodies and hearts, and replenish the soil, our foundation for growth. In winter we are able to reflect and understand things more clearly. We can determine goals, priorities, and plans.

Spring is a time of rebirth for us and all the nature kingdoms. Spring comes softly, heightening our senses and renewing hope for the future. We absorb increasing amounts of light to nourish us. We see new growth and smell the fragrance of the earth as it awakens. We stir and stretch and plan, designing new life through manifestation, thoughts visualized into form.

Summer expands in all directions and asks us to reach out to achieve our fullest potential. It is a time of beauty, bounty, productivity, and gratitude. We encircle ourselves in perpetual energy and move forward on our soul path. The extended daylight hours give us opportunities to plant, play, engage, and create the life we desire, the life we are meant to have.

Fall! How satisfying to reap the fruits of our labors as we rejoice in the abundance of harvest. There is transformation in us and our garden with visible changes in appearance and character. The thoughts, words, and actions of our previous months collectively show up for us to harvest, use, and enjoy. We celebrate the new bounty and abundance, creativity and vision, wishes and dreams as they come to light. We celebrate a new level of maturity, open our arms wide in gratitude, and take time to prepare again for winter to sustain all life.

All four seasons promote our well-being and future growth. Being aware of their purpose allows us to be present to the day and maximize its usefulness and potential.

Discovery Thoughts

Knowing that nature seeks to thrive and rebalance, how do you use each season to rest, rebirth, expand, and reap?

....

Affirmation: "I am one with all cycles of life. Nature restores my energy and balance."

....

Now add an affirmative thought to continue your flow of positive energy: "I . . ."

....

Nourishment

*"You, sent out beyond your recall,
go to the limits of your longing."*

—Rainer Maria Rilke

All living things require nourishment to promote multidimensional growth: physical, mental, emotional, and spiritual. Certain nutrients also assist us in protection, immunity, and optimizing well-being by balancing proteins, carbohydrates, fats, vitamins, and liquids. The nourishment we give to ourselves is reflected in the overall health of the garden.

Similarly, self-nurturance, self-esteem, and loving relationships also promote a sense of well-being within us. Experiences in balanced environments promote peace, relaxation, positive thoughts, and acceptance. Releasing negativity and criticism builds trust, confidence, and relationships. As we mature and develop our spiritual life further, we feed our soul with prayer, meditation, gratitude, discovery, and connection with heart and higher self. All of these are reflected in the garden.

Truth, faith, and authenticity nourish our whole being. When we reside in an energetic plane where we strive to live as a whole being, one with higher self and in alignment with who we truly are, we are refreshed with the energy of positivity. Being genuine is an act of faith that nourishes our whole being. It requires that our truth be in alignment with higher self without attachment to ego or fear. To be genuine requires courage, the courage to know that we are unique for a reason, for a purpose, and that we are meant to share our talents and spirit. Courage strengthens us to be willing to discover the depth of ourselves and fulfill our life purpose. We are always rewarded with blessings when we are genuine and are courageous enough to dare to reveal our unique selves.

As an intensive care unit nurse, I was met with life-changing circumstances during almost every shift. This included the patients' fragile state of health as well as my own concentration and ability to recognize heralding signs and symptoms that required intervention. Most often my actions were well laid out within physician orders and protocols, but sometimes there are unforeseen events that required split-second decisions. When I worked in the Philadelphia area, we had a medical and surgical ICU attached to each other with a total of thirty-six beds. In the surgical area, most beds were only divided by a curtain. I was assigned to the surgical area and two very compromised patients.

There was a code, not my patient, in one of the other bays. A code is when someone stops breathing or their heart stops beating. When this happened, people ran over, the code team responded, and one of my patients had a full view of the resuscitation efforts. I drew his curtain over to shield him.

"Don't let them do that to me," he said clearly.

I said something that I thought was reassuring like, "It's okay, you're doing fine," and continued to assess and check him.

"Promise me," he said. "Don't let them do that to me."

I looked up as his monitor alarms went off and showed that his heart had stopped beating. I checked for a pulse and called out automatically for help. "Help! I need help!"

But even as I yelled those words, I wasn't sure what I was asking for. Staff came, and I tried to explain the situation as they began the life-saving intervention processes. I remember begging for them to stop.

"He doesn't want this. He made me promise not to do this to him." He was a "full code," as they say, meaning there was no written order to limit resuscitation efforts. I was committed to following his instructions, however, and I emphasized his mental acuity and awareness and that if time had allowed, I would have called his physician for a change in his orders. They told me to step away and I did.

I blessed him. I prayed for guidance and forgiveness.

After the code ended unsuccessfully, I went back to his bedside and helped others clean up and prepare for the family to come in. The family thanked all of us and mentioned things like, "He was ready to go" and, "He didn't want to live like this." They went to the physician who was writing his notes at the central desk. This was the 1980s. We were not on computers yet. The physician told me later that the family apologized to him for not coming to him sooner. They felt it had been their responsibility to convey their loved one's last requests for his life, and they had not done that.

"I guess that's why you were here," he said to me.

But I had not followed orders and, in fact, had obstructed people who were trying to intervene. At least that's what was written in the incident report. My manager was sympathetic to me on one level but on the other reminded me that I could have lost my license. The physician refused to sign the incident report and instead wrote an order for "Do Not Resuscitate," which he timed a minute or two after the code was called. In his notes he explained the family's communication to him.

I have always considered myself a patient advocate, acting as a voice for those who are vulnerable and promoting their health and wellness. People's last requests are holy water. I am blessed to be part of their journey. I bless them for allowing me to be present with them at this pivotal time. I will always remember this man who gave me the opportunity to fulfill his last wish while guiding me to affirm my authenticity and truth.

Blessings are garden fertilizer for us, and all that is within our spectrum. When you ask for a blessing to be bestowed upon someone or something, you convey sacred energy. You project positive energy with love and generosity. Blessings nourish with the intent to bring goodness forward into the world. You will always receive in kind what you freely share in blessed holiness.

Discovery Thoughts

Pause a moment to breathe in and align with your higher self. What blessing would you send yourself today? What blessing would you send out into the world?

....

Affirmation: "I am a blessing to life. Blessings nourish me with positivity and generosity."

....

Now add an affirmative thought to continue your flow of positive energy: "I . . ."

....

Energy

"As for me, I know nothing else but miracles."

—Walt Whitman

Dynamic energy abounds in life and bathes the Soul Garden. Sunlight, moonlight, starlight—spiritual guidance, cosmic alignment, and the energy of the multidimensions of the universe transmit energy in the form of vibrations. Our seeds and bodies draw this energy inward to transform ourselves. We are energetic beings of divine light and love. We absorb energy, transmute energy, and bestow energy with our thoughts, words, and actions. Because of this energy we can be seen in physical form, but our core is a spiritual being. Our energetic connection elevates us, connecting mind, body, and spirit as one.

Energy also flows to us. Energy brings sustenance and new discoveries. We receive energy from vibrations, intuition, cosmic waves, and subconscious states, such as dreams. Dreams are messages through the subconscious. Ideas and feelings in the conscious mind can surface in dreams, bringing them to a place where we feel safe and secure to explore them. They may be desires of the heart or spiritual messages. Dreams can be discoveries in motion, indicating a time of newness, transition, and change. During subconscious sleep we are open for thoughts to come forward and float through us in channeled multidimensional space.

Manifestation is our ability to create in the physical world using the energy of spirit and intention. We can use our energy to manifest what we want for ourselves and for others. Manifestation combines our mindful thoughts with projected energy as you visualize it to come forward. It is based on the law of attraction and the belief that directed thoughts and energy seek connection with similar entities, with form. Manifestation is envisioning what you desire followed through with affirmative action steps that enable life forces to guide you. Whatever you have thought, said, and acted upon will be answered in some way.

Trust your intuition and your power over the illusions of the physical world. The abilities to create on the earthly plane and in your Soul Garden are the energetic alignment of conscious choice and soul purpose.

"Destiny is the push of our instincts to the pull of our purpose."

—T.D. Jakes

Dynamic energy comes forward to assist us in sensing what is beyond our normal comprehension. Through its connection we can explore and utilize the depth of power it presents to us.

Discovery Thoughts

How do you use the energy of manifestation to create what you desire in life?

....

Affirmation: "I am guided through the wisdom of Spirit. I manifest the life I desire."

....

Now add an affirmative thought to continue your flow of positive energy: "I . . ."

....

Weeding

"A heart that has been broken and seen pain, reveals within it,
a crack that allows more light in."

—Madisyn Taylor

Weeding is clearing and releasing. Every garden requires weeding, certainly once a year or perhaps more often with the frequent changes that occur in life. If you neglect your weeding, your garden grows out of control and it's difficult to distinguish between plants that you want and weeds that you do not need.

Spring, summer, and fall provide opportunities to move through your Soul Garden with careful eyes and hands to keep all the beds in order. Winter allows time for reflection and assessing the past fruitful seasons of growth. Even in winter, reviewing and planning for spring can reveal insights and priorities. If left unattended, weeds will invade and crowd other plants, leaving them vulnerable to disease and garden pests (fears, doubts, insecurities).

It requires conscious effort to look carefully at the true weeds in your life, things that no longer serve you, things that are no longer in balance with who you have become: old habits, beliefs, negativity, judgments, neglect, guilt, and anger.

This is your opportunity to review their growth and make conscious changes.

Sometimes we attach to other people's negative energy and absorb it. Once absorbed it conflicts with our consciousness and ability to balance. This energy can also produce weeds in the garden. Weeding is clearing old energy, burdens that hamper progress in life and on your soul path.

Look into your Soul Garden as an observer and choose where you want to focus attention. All weeds at some point have had a purpose in your life. Remember that at one time most weeds were plants with flowers blooming in their own right. You learned from them, and they influenced you. You may not like a particular plant, but the question is *why*. Plants can be trimmed, moved to different areas, and tended to differently to promote new growth.

Through experiences we sense, feel, perceive, and create mental snapshots. We store them. The meaning we have attached to memories can greatly affect how we live in the present. Expectations of what will occur in the future (like fond memories associated with childhood holidays) may far exceed the reality of what was in the past, and the past can never be recreated in the present. The world is different. We have become different. Knowing that nothing is the same, we can gratefully allow everything to be new. Let your mind be open.

"The past is never where you think you left it."

—Katherine Anne Porter

Do not allow negative experiences to overtake the garden. Weeds grow in a moment of time in conjunction with specific circumstances and are not reflective of the garden as a whole. They may be things that are no longer in your best interest or that you have outgrown.

When negativity grows in a garden, it chokes other plants at their roots. Negativity, the voice of the ego, shows itself as fear, judgments, anger, resentment, and arrogance. Ego and arrogance weeds try to control you, wanting you to remain chained to lower-self energies. Anger, resentment, and judgment weeds try to stifle you, blunting your potential. Thorns, briars, and prickle weeds try to hurt you, subordinating you to give them power. Regardless of why they are there, it now falls on you to clear space and clear the burdens upon you that they have produced.

"True satisfaction with one's life is an acceptance of what is, continuing to prepare for what can be, while letting go of what we thought needed to be."

—Anne Wilson Schaef

Weeding is the conscious release of the past to live in the present and promote new growth. Paying careful attention to what you wish to create allows you to choose what no longer serves you. Weeding can bring clarity to events and situations you had not previously understood. By weeding you release attachment to the weed (event or situation) and your associated emotions.

All weeds can be used as compost, grounding energy back into the earth. Visualize that you are creating a compost pile that will be later transformed to nourish the garden. With respect to their role in promoting experiences and learnings, we bless the weeds in our garden and return them to the earth. As you tend your garden and create your compost beds, remember to bless their worth as they have brought you to this place of higher awareness. Bless their purpose to fertilize new soil with renewed energy.

Discovery Thoughts

What weeds have you consciously removed from your Soul Garden?

....

Affirmation: "I release all that no longer serves me. I ground life energy back into the earth."

....

Now add an affirmative thought to continue your flow of positive energy: "I . . ."

....

Transplantation and Propagation

"Help us to be ever faithful gardeners of the spirit,
who know that without darkness nothing comes to birth,
and without light nothing flowers."

—May Sarton

The Soul Garden offers us opportunities to recreate our lives. There are two processes in the garden that seek to create new life by moving or using part of the existing plant to create new growth: transplantation and propagation. Through these processes we preserve the energy of the existing plant, our initial seeds and intentions, and we can begin new growth.

Transplantation shifts the plant body to a similar but more beneficial environment within the garden setting or removes it completely from the soil to relocate it. A gardener must carefully consider the phase of growth a plant is in before it is transplanted, remembering that grounded energy from the roots will always remain in the earth.

We can also see transplantation in the physical world when we choose a new job or career. Our work life is reflective of our desire to contribute and be of benefit to the world. When we accept new work, we are exchanging environments, expectations, and opportunities for new growth.

Propagation seeks to multiply the attributes of the plant by direct use of the plant body rather than using its seeds. Spiritually, propagation is giving of the self, an act of service. Propagation always creates new opportunities for growth.

Propagation is akin to changes in life circumstances wherein you retain part of you as you are in the present while giving another part to a higher purpose. Examples of this would be marriage or divorce or taking vows to join a convent. You are beginning anew while still residing in the garden as before.

> *"Each morning we are born again.*
> *What we do today is what matters most."*
>
> —Jack Kornfield, *Buddha's Little Instruction Book*

The choice to transplant and propagate are conscious choices. We may desire to replicate what the plant has offered us or move it to a different location within the garden to enhance its growth. Perhaps we recognize something that was rewarding and successful years before and desire that it be added to our current plantings.

It is important in both these processes to understand what traits you want to duplicate and why. Circumstances and environments change over time and may not support the new growth you desire.

What are you leaving behind? Is it part of the plant or just the roots? Part of your growth will always remain in its original location. Whichever method you choose, be gentle. The plant is an offshoot of yourself and will do best with encouragement and nurturing.

And lastly, as a spiritual gardener, bless your intentions and actions.

Discovery Thoughts

Think of an experience in your life when you transplanted or propagated yourself. What did you create in the new environment?

....

How would you choose to transform yourself?

....

Affirmation: "I create new growth with change. I multiply that which I divide."

....

Now add an affirmative thought to continue your flow of positive energy: "I . . ."

....

Chapter 8
Healing

"To one who waits, all things reveal themselves so long as you have the courage not to deny in the darkness what you have seen in the light."

—Coventry Patmore

Healing is a gift of restoration and regeneration. It is a process of growth. It restores us to a new state of well-being and enables us to regenerate and revive systems, connections, and layers (depth) that assist us in growth, balance, and realignment. While healing is unique to each of us and each situation, it follows the same process every time. We heal physically, mentally, emotionally, and spiritually from the inside, to affect changes. Healing is connective. Our well-being depends on the alignment of the mind, body, and spirit.

Healing as a Process

"Sometimes a person has to go back, really back—to have a sense, an understanding of all that's gone to make them—before they can go forward."

—Paule Marshall

The need to heal may or may not be obvious to you. Physical wounds of the body are usually more obvious. They bleed or swell or cause pain. Pain from any source at any level is a sign that something is not in alignment and requires healing.

Other signs that healing is needed are not as obvious and may be rooted in the mind, emotions, the physical being, and even the spiritual self. We may choose to ignore these signs or believe they will go away on their own, but our physical being has an ingenious reminder system. If you miss the clues, they come again! Unfortunately, they also tend to worsen over time.

All outward signs of illness have a corresponding inward connection. Fever, cough, and headache may indicate pneumonia of the lungs. Likewise, inward causes of illness have a corresponding outward presentation. Multiple areas of bruising on the skin without injury may represent a coagulation dysfunction. Unresolved negative feelings can become deeply rooted and eventually present as physical symptoms or a physical problem. The burdens of negativity (despair, depression, anger, resentment) are too heavy to carry over time and may be expressed in isolation, anxiety, malaise, or outbursts. Self-reflection in the Soul Garden allows you to see and understand where healing is needed.

Healing is change, and change is a process. Change is meant to bring you back into balance and alignment. Obstacles and forces of resistance that you encounter are meant to be guiding messages, to help you see what is lacking or needs to be released. Relationship issues can point to dysfunctional communication problems, for instance, showing a lack of honesty and openness between people. Recurring patterns and experiences display unfinished issues, encouraging you to explore them once more. Be conscious of your truth and any deviations from it. Deviations are illusions rising from ego mind meant to distract you and give rise to doubt yourself. Self-esteem, self-worth, and authenticity are important to overall health and healing.

Biological dysfunction eventually becomes visible in all planes. All parts of our being—physical, mental, emotional, and spiritual—need to be simultaneously cared for in both the earthly and spiritual planes for the healing process to maintain the integrity of our systems. The body and mind in the earthly plane create outcome-oriented healing by monitoring and initiating physiological and psychological responses to regain physical homeostasis. Physical symptoms, such as hives, are indications of allergic biological changes that guide us to make or seek interventions that are required for health.

On the spiritual plane, the spiritual self desires to share in the wisdom of the higher self. It requires that the mind be open to listen and allow the flow of healing thoughts to come forward. Imagine a stream of sacred water rising from your higher self and flowing into your body. Feel its soothing sensations as it washes away all aspects of negativity and fear. The stream flows in a continuous motion with your thoughts. Healing energy is infinite.

Healing is not a cure, and the word "cure" is misleading. It implies a finality while healing is ongoing every day of our lives. The body knows intrinsically how to heal. Healing is a continuous process of four steps: discovery, recovery, change, and opportunity.

Four Steps of Healing

1. **Discovery:** In the discovery step, we uncover what has deviated from our normal. It is an aspect of "dis-ease," as Louise Hay has taught us, and a state we are not comfortable to remain in.

   We begin by acknowledging the condition or situation and then identifying what we feel is needing corrective action. We choose to take action steps or not. Discovery can be a long process, and it is influenced by our ability to accept that we need to investigate further. Beyond that initial realization, the speed at which we can meet with resources to determine our needs and begin a treatment plan may vary greatly. We may deny the findings or believe that if more time is given, things will resolve on their own. This of course may happen, but postponement of discovery processes is often an aspect of denial. Rooted in fear, denial does not open channels for healing. Discovery can be very complicated and affects our emotions, ego, power, faith, and trust.

2. **Recovery:** Recovery is a time of rebalance and recuperation. We can assess our progress over time, utilize the help of others, and adjust our daily lives to move forward in our healing. Often recovery includes making compromises in how we are accustomed to doing things. Healing is a natural state of being. We are always healing. Throughout this step we continue to move closer to our goals of repairing our health and well-being. In recovery we become more aware of the impact that disease and other conditions have had upon our life and may continue to have upon our life. Depending on the source of our dis-ease, we need to pay attention to releasing any negativity and burdens we have carried during this time. This includes feelings and memories associated with pain, despair, regret, and anger, to mention a few.

3. **Change:** This step is the recognition and initiation of further internal and external modifications that align with a healthier life and lifestyle. These changes can be temporary or permanent. This step of reassessment and implementation will continue as more changes occur because of our healing. Therefore, changes are meant to help us progress toward goals and wellness. Change is a continuum of awareness, acceptance, and action.

4. **Opportunity:** Opportunities to heal exist in every step on the recovery pathway. They may arise with a deeper understanding of an initial problem or the continued revisions that strengthen our abilities and resolve. Opportunities exist every day. When you are compromised, these opportunities can become more visible as you look for alternatives to things affecting you or limiting you.

When you think of healing what comes to mind? Often, we think it will be a return to previous functionality and ability—to be what we once were. But healing is always moving us forward to live our life fully and to the best of our ability. Healing will bring us to a new level of self and new understanding. Is healing visible? Is it tangible? Do you want others to know that you are in a healing process?

Taking steps to heal begins a renewal process like planting a seed in your garden. In time, there are signs that affirm your actions and encourage continuation. Support from others may provide you with additional strength while you reserve your energy for the healing process. Healing also provides an opportunity to ask for help. Asking for help is not a weakness. Asking for help allows others to join in your truth and share their love.

Since 2018, I have actively been in healing processes post-spinal surgeries, as I mentioned before. Although my healing was primarily related to a physical problem, it also encompassed a large amount of my mind and spirit. What I didn't share earlier is that I have required a total of five spinal surgeries between 2018 and 2025. The first four surgeries focused on my lumbar spine degeneration and compression fractures to resolve left-leg paralysis. My fifth and most serious surgery involved my cervical spine to correct spinal cord injury and myelopathy from further bone degeneration, compression, and fractures.

Degeneration can occur with disease processes such as systemic arthritis and osteoporosis. The spine is a lever, and repeated flexion, especially with weight-bearing activities, erodes the bone. I am aware that as a nurse I lifted and carried many patients over decades of time. Although my nursing career and general aging have probably been significant in impacting my spinal health, my degenerative condition was not necessarily predictable or preventable. I understand that my genetic makeup, just the way I am, underlies this continuing evolving condition.

My healing is a continuous process of walking the steps and pathway of growth and recovery before me. I am an avid flower gardener, a master gardener. I am also a nurse who has been involved in direct patient care for more than thirty-five years.

Back soreness? A way of life.

Diminishing ability to walk quickly due to left leg weakness? Maybe muscle strain. Annoying. Keep going.

Progressively increasing leg and back pain? Decreasing feeling and sensation? Heralding signs. Go to doctor. Do not pass go.

During the COVID-19 pandemic, I had to wait several months each time to get on the operative schedule. I required a walker. I could not drive. My family fully supported me.

My son ordered groceries online and delivered them to me. He often cooked. My daughter-in-law found a wonderful person who cleaned my house. All of what was part of my daily routine changed. I began to not recognize myself. I felt angst over what I was not capable of doing anymore. "Just write" was the message I continued to receive in prayer. "Just write."

I experienced many dark days of extreme pain, sadness, and doubt. When I froze in this fear my son would repeatedly say to me, "This is just one day, Mum. This is not the rest of your life."

I held on to that statement with both hands and veered away from the many unknowns that plagued me. I faithfully adopted a focused concentration in living one day at a time. When my mind would wander to dark places of fear, I would ask myself, "Is this a question I need to answer today?" If it wasn't, then I wrote it down on a piece of paper, folded it over several times, and literally put it in a shoebox to think about in the future. The more egregious the question, the more I folded the paper to its smallest size.

One day, each day. You can do it one day at a time. Each new day is God's gift to you.

As I recovered each time after surgery, my joy was relief from the pain in my back and leg. The surgical pain was nothing compared to the pre-op pain. My greatest fear was that I would not be able to regain full functioning of my leg. I needed to learn how to walk again, to balance, and to stand straight.

I had to remind myself frequently that recovery is a process. That goals are future-thinking and will modify as healing occurs. That time is a human measurement, not a spiritual one.

I got out of bed every day. I utilized all the services available to me. I continued physical therapy. I eventually reached a level of functionality where I could be mostly independent. I was gratefully able to connect with friends. I kept going.

Prayer and meditation were daily conversations I looked forward to. I kept writing.

There are changes required to achieve what you *have* to do and changes to achieve what you *want* to do. There are changes you cannot make by yourself, and you must ask for help. I humbly learned to accept all help with gratitude and bless the people who came forward. I wrote about insight, intuition, angelic messages, courage, and strength. I wrote to better understand my feelings and needs. I wrote because every thought is a prayer.

I did not like some of the changes I experienced. In fact, there were times when I resented them even though I knew it was part of a path to progress and healing, and the truth of my healing. I had moments of extreme frustration over what I could no longer do easily or by myself. Frustration, anger, or despair—whatever you want to call them—were dark places.

After each surgery I gradually regained my ability to walk. I cannot turn or twist at my waist. I cannot bend at my waist. When I bend it is from my hips. Balance remains a limitation for me, and I need a cane or walker most of the time. I can drive, which adds a wonderful level of gratitude and a new appreciation for freedom.

Imagine the disappointment I felt when after each surgery, a year to a year and a half later, the symptoms of leg weakness and pain returned. A little further up on my spine, the degenerative process had occurred again.

Surgery was scheduled. I wrote more.

I do believe that everything that happens in your life is happening *for* you, not *to* you.

I searched for meanings and strengthened my faith and belief that all things are possible even if not probable. The time I have been given allows me to write and publish, develop more artistry, and give of myself and my talents to bring more light and love into the world. In my journey I have grown to understand that I was not meant to be given a reason why these things have happened to me. Acceptance is a place of peace.

What we believe about ourselves creates an image of who we are. Own and accept your present life as it is so you can step forward from there. Know that you can continue to create what you desire and what you desire to be. Empower yourself to create the change you wish to embody. Believe in yourself and the holy creation that you are. "Holy" means sacred. Treat yourself as the sacred being you are.

> *"Truly, it is in the darkness that one finds the light, so when we are in sorrow, then this light is nearest to all of us."*
>
> —Meister Eckhart

Emotional Healing

Emotional healing, the healing of the interpretations of the mind inward to the heart, is a delicate process of unveiling and accepting. It is possibly the most difficult type of healing because we become invested in how we feel through connections with our mind and ego.

The wounds of the emotions are personal injuries, embedded on a visceral level. Personal wounds leave scars that need to be reabsorbed so they can be loved as we love ourselves. Scars restrict us from fully expanding to experience higher levels of trust.

The psychiatrist Carl Jung described a "personal unconsciousness" within us that is overridden with feelings, emotions, and memories of the past, both light and dark. These creations of the mind implant themselves into our psyche and can be triggered to seep back into consciousness as if they were happening anew.

Emotional healing requires the mind to separate the event from the reaction, our emotional response. What we remember is the story. What we felt is the emotional response. Memories are our perceptions of the past and may not reflect what actually happened. Releasing is a process of consciously emptying the personal unconsciousness to fill it with the goodness that you are and that you desire. Fear can become trust; anger can embrace love. Be willing to delete your story, your perceptions of the event, and other people's actions—what you cannot change. Your present feelings, not the past, are the key to regaining personal power.

Whatever we feel is a legitimate response of the wounded self. Like fight or flight, we make instantaneous decisions to react, then assess and reevaluate our true feelings later. There is no magic Band-Aid that will take away the pain of deep wounds. We are left to uncover the rawness and work toward regaining balance, alignment, and wholeness. The mind is a wizard of connivance, and statements like "I should have known better" grasp at illusions of control. These ego-based recriminations bury truth even deeper, and truth and authenticity are the steppingstones to moving forward.

Healing Pain

There are many types of pain, multiple ways it can be felt, and many degrees of severity. Experiencing pain can feel uncomfortable to unbearable. Expressing your pain can range from silence to moaning to screaming. Like our emotions, it is how we feel that dictates a response.

Physical pain is processed by the mind through nerve stimulation. Nerves send sensations through conduction passageways to the brain to be translated. Our first reactions are to withdraw (move away from), cry out (express feelings), and then look at ways to repair our body.

The amount of time that is required for pain to heal, diminish, or go away is very variable and very personal. Some people can tolerate higher levels of pain sensation. Some people may have anticipatory pain, meaning that they expect a certain level of pain associated with the event prior to the event. A clear example of this is when children react to having a shot before it is given.

There are many ways to work with pain to reduce its impact. Medications include pills and ointments; ice packs and hot packs; dressings to reduce the exposure of the wound; and meditative breathing. Breathing as a focus, slowly and evenly, reduces pain.

I have experienced many levels of pain and have the utmost compassion for those feeling pain. Constant unrelieved pain disrupts sleep, can cause depression, and erodes faith.

Grief is a type of pain that occurs as a result of a loss. You can feel loss on many levels: personal, professional, psychological, physical, spiritual, and material. Healing grief is a continuum of releasing emotions and replenishing yourself through nourishment and nurturance. Feelings of insecurity may arise with loss of home, loss of a partner, and loss of income. This insecurity adds another dimension of stress and fear to the process of grief. When grief is stored, it becomes a burden that is carried every day, and it is not easily released.

Stress is a condition of fear. Fear is disruptive to all natural processes and is an obstacle to actualizing a higher-self state. Constantly living in stress is an attempt to incorporate unhealthy patterns into our being and into our lives to preserve something we feel has value. The value we place upon an entity dictates the level of stress we are willing to accept and attempt to manage. Insecurity, low self-esteem, and fear of abandonment may underlie the need to live in stressful environments, where we believe we are less than others and less than what we expect of ourselves. What is "expected" of us arises from external and internal forces and creates illusions of the ego-mind. Fear is disruptive to all natural processes and prevents us from actualizing our highest self.

Forgiveness of ourselves and others is a choice we make to release burdens and achieve freedom from negativity. Forgiveness is essential to our well-being. Our self-care includes forgiving ourselves, releasing aspects of control, and allowing the power of healing energy to restore us. When we judge others, we create negativity and blame. The ego feels we have been wronged and expects compensation. By forgiving, an action of the heart, we accept what has occurred as a factual event. We are not condoning it but choosing instead to repel the burden of its negativity in our life. Staying focused in the present is key to regaining balance and alignment. By choosing to be free, you are choosing to live with light and love in peace and harmony. You are allowing yourself to love fully as intended.

All experiences, even painful ones, are learning opportunities. What you experienced eventually brought you to the place you are now. Ask yourself what you learned from it. How did you grow? Is there anything remaining that is toxic to your life and future?

*"All we are asked to bear we can bear. That is a law of spiritual life.
The only hindrance to the working of this law,
as of all benign laws, is fear."*

—Elizabeth Goudge

Discovery Thoughts

In what areas of your life have you experienced healing?

....

Emotional healing requires that we empty our personal unconsciousness. What remains in this aspect of your mind that you wish to release?

....

What does forgiveness mean to you? Is there anything in your life you feel needs forgiveness?

....

Affirmation: "I embody the flow of higher-self energy. I live in health and wholeness."

....

Now add an affirmative thought to continue your flow of positive energy: "I . . ."

....

Energetic Healing

*"The child is an almost universal symbol for the soul's transformation.
The child is whole, not yet divided. . . . When we would heal the mind
. . . we ask this child to speak to us."*

—Susan Griffin

The natural order of life is to heal and return the mind, body, and spirit to a state of balance and alignment. We are in a perpetual course of recalibration. Healing is an active process. It is life and growth nourished at the same time. Unresolved issues with emotional gravity and guilt have a strong magnetic energy attraction and attract situations with the same vibration.

We transmit energy attached to our thoughts, words, and actions as an active process. Thus, we have responsibility for them. We create vibrational energy with our actions, acceptance, and love. When we bless something or someone, we convey positive energy upon them. Offer blessings to yourself and for your healing, and to all others who assist you.

We are also able to receive energy from other people and living things at all times. It is important to separate yourself from the energies of others, especially any negative energy. Negative energy from others disrupts and complicates the healing process.

Therapeutic energetic healing practices include Reiki therapy. Reiki is energetic healing based on the Japanese methods developed by Dr. Usui from ancient Tibetan texts. "Reiki" means universal life force—the healing energy of the universe. In Reiki sessions, trained individuals assess the energy pathways within your body and through them sense balance and imbalance. Treatments include balancing and releasing energy that is not healthy or helping you. As the Reiki practitioner's hands move above your body, healing energy flows through your chakra energy centers to promote balance and harmony through all dimensions of your being. Reiki can reveal information that points to areas of your body and mind that are misaligned and lead you to insightful physical and spiritual discoveries.

The processes of healing require awareness and participation. Envision yourself releasing any pain and illness. Envision a golden white light flowing down through your crown chakra to illuminate you with the goodness and wellness of healing energy. Allow the light to float over you and through you, collecting all fragments of imbalance and washing them away, all the way down your body and through the soles of your feet to ground back to Mother Earth. Frequently practice seeing this clearing taking place and your healing occurring.

Angelic healing is energy transmitted to you when you ask for help from the angels, guides, archangels, and specific masters. They have guidance over aspects of your life, and you can call upon them for general assistance in areas of need. When you ask for divine intervention, you are evoking spiritual help. Those requests are prayers, and prayer is always answered in your highest good and for the highest good of all. Healing is occurring whether results are palpable to you or not. Always thank the angels for assisting you and for revealing to you what you need to know. Angelic healing is compassionate healing through the heart.

Energetic healing occurs in multiple dimensions on many physical and spiritual planes. It is the flow of positive vibration within us, through us, and from us to reestablish alignment and well-being. With the blessings of divine grace, we open ourselves to vibrational healing energy forces.

Discovery Thoughts

How do you incorporate the flow of universal energy into your life?

....

How does positive energy promote your well-being?

....

Affirmation: "I am an open receptive channel of divine healing energy. I give thanks and gratitude for my health and wellness."

....

Now add an affirmative thought to continue your flow of positive energy: "I . . ."

....

Replenishment

"This is the art of courage: to see things as they are and still believe that the victory lies not with those who avoid the bad, but those who taste, in living awareness, every drop of the good."

—Victoria Lincoln

As we heal, we replenish our mind, body, and spirit from life storms, illness, trauma, emotional gravity, and misalignment. Healing restores our body's reserves and rebalances us in all realms of mind, body, and spirit. When we are healing, we use our physical, mindful, and spiritual energies to fuel the processes. There are countless ways to replenish our energy. It is in our best interest to seek those who are healthy and help us maintain balance and promote regrowth and wellness.

Breathing is the movement of air and associated energy in and out of the body. It is our first physiological action at birth and our last purposeful action at the time of our physical death and transition. Breathing is essential to saving life. Think of CPR and healing therapies that require oxygen.

Our nervous system automatically adjusts our breathing to meet physical and psychological demands. In times of stress, exercise, illness, or fear, the rate and depth of our breathing change to deliver more oxygen and release more carbon dioxide. These processes compensate for altered physiological states and work to rebalance our metabolic state. Breathing has been studied and taught for centuries to promote relaxation, meditation, prayer, and increased oxygenation. We can learn to adjust our breathing accordingly. For example, slow deep breaths are calming and promote realignment as we exhale negativity and fear from within.

Think of the benefits of inhalation and those of exhalation. You will breathe whether you are aware of it or not; it is autonomic. When you consciously breathe you become aware of the rate and depth. You can make your breaths slower or faster. You are more aware of your thoughts and mindfulness. You can sense a shift into relaxation.

Breathing is a wonderful exercise to regain balance. Visualize bringing forward that which you desire in your life and breathe out that which does not serve you. Breathe with awareness until you feel a sense of serenity within you. Build your inner strength with its movement and consistency. Focus on components of your abilities that you use to create goodness in the world. Consciously remove all obstacles to your authenticity and truth.

Release any barriers to the flow of energy within you. Resist attachment to the emotions and actions of others and allow them to own and be responsible for their feelings and behaviors.

Maintaining balance and replenishing reserves allows you to connect with who you truly are, one with higher self. For you are the blessed incarnation of God's love. Know and understand this as the miracle it is!

There are practices you can initiate to facilitate healing processes and your overall health. They rely on your ability to allow processes to occur in their own time and release any constraints we may impose upon ourselves. Bless yourself and your actions. Care for yourself in a loving, respectful, compassionate way. Care for your inner child, the part of you that still exists and waits uninhibitedly to play again. Remember how that child encouraged you, supported you, and comforted you. Remember your innocence. Remember that you are born with purpose in the life you have chosen. Open your wings and give flight!

Practice relaxation as part of your daily replenishment. Find in each day:

* The gift of rest
* The gift of silence
* The gift of listening in the dark, in the void
* The gift of beginning again

Spend time in your Soul Garden. Walk between your plants and blossoms. Notice what you have created and give thanks. State affirmations that reinforce your value and what you want to manifest. Bless yourself and your intentions.

> *"I will love the light for it shows the way, yet I will endure the darkness because it shows me the stars."*
>
> —Og Mandino

Replenishment is a necessary component of nourishment and nurturance. We facilitate this by choosing to rest and reflect, breathing in what we desire, and breathing out what we wish to release. By replenishing we create more room in the garden for positivity, love, and spiritual oneness.

Rest. Relax. Receive. Replenish.

Discovery Thoughts

How do you replenish yourself each day?

....

Being playful and imaginative fosters the innocence of our inner child to resurface. How would you choose to experience the freedom of your inner child again?

....

Affirmation: "I am freedom and self-empowerment. I breathe with life's energy."

....

Now add an affirmative thought to continue your flow of positive energy: "I . . ."

....

Chapter 9

Life Paths

"Sometime in your life you will go on a journey.
It will be the longest journey you have ever taken.
It is the journey to find yourself."

—Katherine Sharp

Pathways

You are on a spiritual journey, and your life is filled with endless possibilities.

Our minds envision opportunities from which we create limitless abundance, health, and happiness. Life is a series of pathways linked together, and our path is a process of continuous growth. All experiences provide learning and expansion. Some learnings bring us joy and hope for the future while others are meant to bring enlightenment, to engage our consciousness in awareness and determining best choices. They give insight through experiences into what is needed to create a more positive and loving life.

How we view the results of our learnings is a personal assessment. A positive view reinforces behavior, while a negative view raises questions in our mind and may cause doubt and concern. All paths in our garden are connected by thought and intention, and we are always where we need to be. We cannot go backward and eliminate an outcome or have a do-over, but we can retrace our steps to gain a broader understanding and a higher-self perspective of our actions and results. The higher self will always see you and your situations from a place of divine love. This includes forgiveness for yourself and others. Seeing all paths through the eyes of divine love is the highest perspective we can hold.

We are reminded again in this chapter how similar everything is created as a process in divine order and divine timing. This occurs both in the garden and in the lives we live. Walking our pathways follows defined processes, and we continually grow, learn, and expand as we walk forward and live our journey. The Soul Garden grows outward from the Tree of Life, lined by circular pathways, each representing a phase of life, a phase of growth. All paths are connected by thought and intention.

In walking our paths, we consciously proceed in a direction, each step building upon all others. Each day has purpose in our life. Destinations evolve and there are side roads, stopping points, and detours. No matter where we have traveled, we are not far from our Tree of Life, our centering point. All paths lead us back to where we need to be.

The garden is a quantum field in which anything can be produced with manifested energy. There is unlimited space and an absence of measured time. As you walk your path in reflection, choose to consciously step forward without attachment and allow the universal flow of energy to come to you. Pathways join the gardens of our life's journeys. Walk in cadence to the mantra of "relax, release, receive, replenish."

Relax into the cadence of your walk. One step, one step, one step. Notice how the birds sing, the wind rustles, and the shadows of the sun fall into pace with you.

Release all stress, negativity, and regrets. Release all that is no longer of value to your life, all that is not in your best interest.

Receive the flow of energy coming to you. Open your mind, your heart, and your senses. Listen to the voice within.

Replenish with the guidance and love that is offered to you by the divine. Feel its warmth as it fills your being and overflows to all that surrounds you.

"We cannot stop the winter or the summer from coming. We cannot stop the spring or the fall or make them other than they are. They are gifts from the universe that we cannot refuse. But we can choose what we will contribute to life when each arrives."

—Gary Zukav

Discovery Thoughts

Visualize walking your life paths in the Soul Garden. How has one path led to the other? How have these paths brought you to the place where you are now?

....

Affirmation: "My journey is spiritually guided. Divine light illuminates my soul path."

....

Now add an affirmative thought to continue your flow of positive energy: "I . . ."

....

Soul Purpose

"The two most important days of your life are the day you were born and the day you find out why."

—Modern Proverb

Soul purpose is the subject of much searching, writing, and discussion. Many people feel it is an elusive state of consciousness, a sacred mystery not easily understood or attained. Some believe that to realize soul purpose we must go through the depths of darkness and strife. But I believe that nothing so beautiful would ever be that complicated. The intention of soul purpose is for us to search for a place of service and belonging, a place that brings happiness to our daily life.

There is no specific age at which we begin to understand where we belong in the world, though we begin to ask relevant questions in early years. Some of us hear a higher calling coming from a place where we are meant to be of service for the greater good. Others will move forward believing they are well suited for a career or position or may accept it out of convenience or sense of duty. Along life's pathway we continue to search, ask for assistance, and receive guidance. Listening to your inner voice, the higher self, is critical to finding soul purpose.

Soul purpose is not a stagnant way of living. It may expand and change throughout the phases and circumstances of our life. It is the relationship of mind, body, and spirit in synchronicity.

People living their soul purpose live varied lives. They may be mothers, fathers, cafeteria workers, nurses, teachers, or artists. They may work in law enforcement, libraries, food banks, or churches. They are energized by their work and feel a calling to it. They intrinsically feel they are right where they belong. Even on the hard days, the days of sadness and disappointment, they know they are making a difference in their life and the lives of others. They also know that without that role they would feel incomplete. They receive something more through their purpose. Something they belong to with their heart.

Why is belonging important? A sense of belonging is fundamental to so many things we do in life. It motivates us, rewards us, and encourages us. When we belong, we feel that we own part of the relationship, part of the work, and part of the rewards. We adopt responsibility. Through the work that we do a sense of our true self emerges. When you are authentic in this way, you align with higher self. Higher self requires authenticity.

Traditionally, teenage years are adventurous and a time of discovery. The lessons we learn during those years have lasting impact on what we believe about the world, ourselves, and others. They influence our future. As we grow, experience, and expand we can restructure, build upon previous foundations, and strengthen the knowledge of who we truly are. In our garden we seed new plants that are heartier and more disease resistant to promote optimal new growth and well-being.

Discovering where you belong, your soul purpose, is a process. There are some people who receive a calling early in their life. Mother Teresa, for example, proceeded to diligently and selflessly honor her calling. For most of us, we proceed on a path that appears open for us, and from that path gain information, skill, and a level of satisfaction. As we discover more, we know more and proceed further.

I graduated from college with a degree in behavior and child development and then became a registered nurse in 1976. I started my career in labor and delivery, then emergency departments, and expanded into intensive care in 1983 when I moved from Louisiana to New Jersey. I was overwhelmed, scared, and totally engrossed in a world of healthcare where every aspect of the patient's physical and mental well-being was in jeopardy. My aha moment was when I realized that the depth of my knowledge and the range of my actions was now intrinsically woven with the life of another. I knew I had found my home. I belonged there. I dedicated my life to ensuring that the care I gave came from a place of competence and compassion, and I prayed for guidance every day.

The ability to make choices always remains within our control, within our ability to analyze and assess. Choice is a God-given blessing. Inner voice will always send messages to guide you. You know what that is. You either feel exhilaration or queasiness. Right?

Listening to your inner guidance reinforces your thinking and your beliefs. Inner guidance conveys positive energy and indicates areas of imbalance. Imbalance may be the message that asks you to make changes in yourself or in your behavior. Imbalance may suggest to you that you belong somewhere else and that it is time to broaden your search. It may suggest that your soul purpose is still waiting for you to find it.

Messages from Spirit also guide us in divine order and divine timing. These communications come through prayer, meditation, mentors, and universal laws. They ask us to extend ourselves and do something more, something beyond our current reach.

In making life-purpose choices there are three paths, three choices you can make to continue your journey:

* You can choose to move forward in faith and promise that your soul purpose will be shown to you and you will fulfill it.

* You can remain uncomfortable in your present situation (even if temporary). This includes going through the motions you have adopted to stay.

* You can step back, retreat, to a previous situation and way of thinking, step back to the same obstacles and a role that did not fulfill you but that was familiar.

What is this process of finding life purpose? You must look. When you are open and willing to look, you are putting a discovery process in motion. This allows opportunities to present themselves, more guidance to come forward, and openings for your intuition and heart to speak to you. Soul purpose is a process of discovery on life's journey. When life purpose is connected to higher self-thinking it forms soul purpose. By allowing opportunities and changes to come into our life, we open ourselves to their gifts. Connect with your higher self. Listen to your intuition and let your heart speak to you.

What is the discovery process? In the discovery process we look for something different for a variety of reasons. Choices we make can reflect our needs, the needs of family and those dependent on us, or the constraints associated with our current situation (insurance, pay level, etc.). We can make choices out of necessity. Trust that necessity guides you to a place of consciousness. In this place of awareness, think of your role and choices as steps forward toward something. Your actions will become clearer and more defined. As you continue to walk further, planting your seeds, things continue to evolve, circumstances change, and opportunities arise.

Your thoughts and questions promote inner guidance and messages. From thoughts come answers. From possibilities come openings. All thoughts are prayers. All prayers are answered. Possibilities are opportunities and opportunities offer growth and change.

Ask yourself, "Do I want more? Am I open to making changes to experience more?"

"The journey of enlightenment is a journey of the mind: from a focus on the body to a focus on spirit, from a limited sense of self to an unlimited sense of Self, from a sense of separateness to a sense of unity with all things. . . . "

—Marianne Williamson

Imagine that you are looking at yourself from two perspectives, above and below.

From above you are your higher self, seeing your spiritual gifts, the desires of your heart, the blessings in your life, and the contributions you have made and want to make in the world. From this point of view, what do you see? What comes to mind?

From above, we can identify areas in our life that ask for more.

Ask yourself, "What are the desires of my heart?" And then ask, "Am I pursuing those desires?"

From below, you are an objective observer.

From this viewpoint, you can identify the factors that influence your choices. Ask yourself, "Am I still that person who wanted these choices? Are those still my desires? Are they still in my best interest?"

Assess what you do, whether you like it or not, and the decisions you make each day.

Know that you will continue to be guided and that your soul path, your higher-self guidance, desires to reconcile any differences between above and below. Ask for universal and divine guidance, clarity, and assistance. Look for signs that reinforce your knowledge of where you belong. Look for wisdom and learnings from the laws of the universe and spiritual laws, showing your relationship, order, and attraction.

Search for the place where you fully engage your talents and are a positive, honest, compassionate dynamic in service to the greater good. Feeling that you are being urged to do something different in your life brings new thought into your awareness. It opens energetic pathways and heightens all your senses. Along with this, as you age, you may begin to consider whatever time you feel you have left in your life. This can motivate you to move in a certain direction believing that if you are going to make a change, to align with something different, it should be sooner rather than later. It's a good time to pause and reflect. Your decisions should come from a place of trust and not fear.

"Ask, and it shall be given you; seek, and ye shall find;
knock, and it shall be opened unto you."

—Matthew 7:7 (NKJV)

Own the decisions you have made while solidifying future choices that align with purpose. Every thought, every step, every choice is a step forward in recognizing and sharing your gifts, in opening fully.

You are your soul, the truth of who you are.

Discovery Thoughts

What do you believe is your soul purpose? How are you living that purpose?

....

Affirmation: "I am a light worker. I bring greater good into the world."

....

Now add an affirmative thought to continue your flow of positive energy: "I ..."

....

Soul Path

"There is only one thing you should do. Go into yourself."

—Rainer Maria Rilke

Our paths have led us back to the center of our garden. Here we are standing beneath our Tree of Life looking outwardly once again on the beautiful creations in this life and in our lifetimes. Your soul path is all the pathways you are walking, have walked, and will walk. Everything is embedded in the steps you take. Our earthly lives are lived in cycles of divine order: birth, growth, death/transition, and rebirth. You have traveled through these dimensions. They appear repeatedly in the plants you grow in the Soul Garden. With deep roots, you emerge again, to bloom again, to seed again. You have seen the results of seeds planted in your current lifetime and previous lifetimes. You have emerged again as a being of divine light and love.

There is a purpose in just living as a divine being in physical form. We are meant to create more goodness and kindness in the world and to grow in understanding ourselves in relation to our higher self and Spirit.

Is this the understanding you have of your present life? Is this where you are?

Remember that everything is a continuous process of discovery. Look beyond yourself with objectivity and higher-self consciousness. Our experiences urge us to search for and live an expanded life, embracing all that is. Our goals should align with living a life with integrity, harmony, and authenticity.

"I slept and dreamt that life was joy. I awoke and saw that life was service. I acted and behold, service was joy."

—Rabindranath Tagore

We are capable of sensing the needs of others and our universe. We are able to give without expectation of return. To look beyond yourself is a choice of consciousness.

To live with integrity, harmony, and authenticity, we are asked to:

* Align with our higher self and be one with Spirit
* Align with our soul's purpose
* Align with our soul's path

And lastly, with the grace and benevolence of God, everything you need is right inside you. It is already written as you emerged through the veil, waiting to be discovered.

That is the mystery of soul purpose.

Accessing Your Soul Garden

Take in a deep breath, inhaling the fullness of your life. Your Soul Garden is a place where you belong. It is familiar to you.

Your Soul Garden is accessible at any time and from any place. Chakra energy pathways act as conduits to allow us to transcend through our heart space to be one with our spiritual self. Divine energy comes forward as enlightenment to assist you in this journey of discovery.

Accessing our Soul Garden is personal to each of us, but I do believe it requires a form of meditative consciousness. You create this level of meditation and connection.

This book describes one scenario you can use to meditate and reflect upon. As you develop your own entryway, you will find other processes that also work for you.

I encourage you to seek this place of discovery and explore its depths as your true self to be one with higher self and Spirit within your Soul Garden.

"The Promised Land always lies on the other side of a wilderness."

—Havelock Ellis

Learning to access your garden is a conscious process that requires preparation, time, and consistency in a quiet peaceful atmosphere, in harmony with nature and yourself.

Softly close your eyes and take several comfortable slow and deep breaths, in and out, to clear your thoughts. Think of releasing all that is present in your mind. Allow these thoughts to flow from you with exhalation. As you breathe out, bless anything that may be troubling you. Bless its highest good as you let it go. Allow it to find its own path in the universe.

Keeping your eyes closed, allow your breathing to resume a normal depth and balance as it becomes slower and shallower. Your mind continues to clear and sensations flow to you in the space you have created. You are aware from a distance that your body is breathing in what you need and giving out what no longer serves you. Open all your being with immense gratitude.

Your body continues to breathe naturally as you connect with the energy flowing through you. Visualize yourself standing somewhere. Maybe a field or a sandy beach, standing barefoot firmly on the ground, connecting with the earth. And as you are standing there breathing in, you feel the energy and vibration of the Earth, travelling all the way up your legs to your back, coming in through the lower chakras and up to the root, the sacral, the solar plexus in its flowing warmth. You breathe the flow of that energy higher to your chest and heart chakra, anchoring Earth's energy into your heart.

And now feel the energy of the higher realm, the heavenly realm, coming down through your higher chakras, coming down into your crown, connecting you to the divine light of Spirit.

The illumination envelops you knowing it is you, eternal you—you who have travelled through time and space to be in this now moment. Know that you are here to bring forth a beautiful message, one with your soul's purpose as only you can bring forth. In this space know that everything you are and everything you need is contained within the light of this beautiful radiance inside you.

From the top of your head and through your crown chakra, golden light continues to envelop you with its presence. The light expands downward to the center of your forehead to the gateway of the third eye and into a white void in which you become emerged in its vapor. You are one in spiritual light.

You are the light moving downward, past your throat chakra, the source of voice and truth, and into your heart to unite with the grounded light from below.

Breathe in as you move with the flow of golden light deeper into your heart, dropping down into your heart center as if you have entered an expansive room.

Imagine that golden light glowing, spreading outward through all the dimensions of your being, filling every cell and vessel of your body so you are one energy within the light. You are the light that continues to move expansively throughout.

Your heart in its pure golden vibration leads you with the flow of grace, one with Spirit, through the door, the door in the back of your heart.

And you move across the threshold and out into a beautiful field of green, bathed in bright white light, where you become present on a golden pathway.

And you follow the golden pathway across the field and up a small hill to a magnificent tree, a tree taller than your vision, its branches lifting into celestial skies. You reach out and touch its skin, and it breathes with you, you and energy and its energy as one source.

And you see before you beautiful gardens of every plant imaginable. Greens and leaves in patterns, blooms and buds in all colors and heights. Gardens of your making, living forms of your thoughts, experiences, and lifetimes. You rise into the vapors, one with the light and the magnificence of you.

Your journey is a process of loving yourself. Love where you have been, love where you are, and love where you will go. Love that you are growing. Love that you can mature from your experiences and grow again. Love that by loving yourself you can love others for themselves. Love that we are all beings in divine light and love.

I wish you a safe journey in love and light.

Discovery Thoughts

Open your eyes and breathe in the beauty that surrounds you. Describe yourself and what you see.

....

What does the Soul Garden mean to you? Listen to your higher self. What messages come forward?

....

Affirmation: "I am a sacred journey of discovery, acceptance, and love."

....

Now add an affirmative thought to continue your flow of positive energy: "I . . ."

....

"A day dawns, quite like other days; in it, a single hour comes, quite like other hours; but in that day and in that hour the chance of a lifetime faces us."

—Maltbie D. Babcock

Inspirational Resources

Ackerman, Diane. *A Natural History of the Senses*. New York: Random House, 1990.

Baldwin, Christina. *The Seven Whispers: A Spiritual Practice for Times Like These*. Novato, CA: New World Library, 2002.

Ban Breathnach, Sara. *Romancing the Ordinary: A Year of Simple Splendor*. New York: Simple Abundance Press/Scribner, 2002.

Ban Breathnach, Sara. *Simple Abundance: A Daybook of Comfort and Joy*. New York: Warner Books, 1995.

Ban Breathnach, Sara. *Something More: Excavating Your Authentic Self*. New York: Warner Books, 1998.

Barton, Ruth Haley. *Sacred Rhythms: Arranging Our Lives for Spiritual Transformation*. Downers Grove, IL: InterVarsity Press, 2006.

Bernstein, Gabrielle. *Miracles Now: 108 Life-Changing Tools for Less Stress, More Flow, and Finding Your True Purpose*. Carlsbad, CA: Hay House, 2014.

Bernstein, Gabrielle. *The Universe Has Your Back: Transform Fear to Faith*. Carlsbad, CA: Hay House, 2016.

Bolsta, Phil. *Through God's Eyes: Finding Peace and Purpose in a Troubled World*. James Monroe Publishing, 2012.

Borysenko, Joan. *7 Paths to God: The Ways of the Mystic*. Carlsbad, CA: Hay House, 1997.

Borysenko, Joan. *Pocketful of Miracles: Prayers, Meditations, and Affirmations to Nurture Your Spirit Every Day of the Year.* New York: Warner Books, 1994.

Brown, Brené. *Braving the Wilderness: The Quest for True Belonging and the Courage to Stand Alone.* New York: Random House, 2017.

Brown, Brené. *Daring Greatly: How the Courage to Be Vulnerable Transforms the Way We Live, Love, Parent, and Lead.* New York: Avery Publishing, 2012.

Brown, Brené. *The Gifts of Imperfection: Let Go of Who You Think You're Supposed to Be and Embrace Who You Are.* Center City, MN: Hazelden, 2010.

Cameron, Julia. *The Artist's Way: A Spiritual Path to Higher Creativity.* New York: Jeremy P. Tarcher/Penguin, 2002.

Cameron, Julia. *Blessings: Prayers and Declarations for a Heartful Life.* New York: Jeremy P. Tarcher/Penguin, 1998.

Cameron, Julia. *Finding Water: The Art of Perseverance.* New York: Jeremy P. Tarcher/Penguin, 2006.

Cameron, Julia. *Heart Steps: Prayers and Declarations for a Creative Life.* New York: Jeremy P. Tarcher/Penguin, 1997.

Cameron, Julia. *Prayers to the Great Creator: Prayers and Declarations for a Meaningful Life.* New York: Jeremy P. Tarcher/Penguin, 2008.

Cameron, Julia. *Transitions: Prayers and Declarations for a Changing Life.* New York: Jeremy P. Tarcher/Penguin, 1999.

Cameron, Julia, and Emma Lively. *The Prosperous Heart: Creating a Life of "Enough."* New York: Jeremy P. Tarcher/Penguin, 2011.

Casey, Karen. *Each Day a New Beginning: Daily Meditations for Women*. Center City, MN: Hazelden, 1982.

Chittister, Joan. *The Breath of the Soul: Reflections on Prayer*. New London, CT: Twenty-Third Publications, 2009.

Chittister, Joan. *The Gift of Years: Growing Older Gracefully*. New York: BlueBridge, 2008.

Chittister, Joan. *The Monastic Way*. www.monasticway.org.

Chopra, Deepak. *The Seven Spiritual Laws of Success: A Practical Guide to the Fulfillment of Your Dreams*. San Rafael, CA: Amber-Allen Publishing/New World Library, 1994.

Crowley, Hilary McCann. *The Power of Energy Medicine*. New York: Skyhorse, 2021.

Dyer, Wayne W. *Change Your Thoughts—Change Your Life: Living the Wisdom of the Tao*. Carlsbad, CA: Hay House, 2007.

Dyer, Wayne W. *Happiness Is the Way: How to Reframe Your Thinking and Work with What You Already Have to Live the Life of Your Dreams*. Carlsbad, CA: Hay House, 2019.

Dyer, Wayne W. *The Power of Intention: Learning to Co-Create Your World Your Way*. Carlsbad, CA: Hay House, 2004.

Dyer, Wayne W. *You Are What You Think: 365 Meditations for Extraordinary Living*. Carlsbad, CA: Hay House, 2018.

Edkins, Janet, CEO. Jay Designs Inc. Web Design. Knoxville, TN. jaydesignsinc.com.

Hay, Louise. *Heart Thoughts: A Treasury of Inner Wisdom*. Carlsbad, CA: Hay House, 2012.

Holmes, Ernest. *Creative Ideas: A Spiritual Compass for Personal Expression*. Burbank, CA: Science of Mind Publishing, 2009.

Jones, Carolyn A., Energy Architect. The Holistic Institute of Wellness. Summerville, SC. holisticinstituteofwellness.com.

Merton, Thomas. *A Year with Thomas Merton: Daily Meditations from His Journals*. Selected and edited by Jonathan Montaldo. San Francisco, CA: HarperOne, 2004.

Millman, Dan. *The Four Purposes of Life: Finding Meaning and Direction in a Changing World*. Novato, CA: H. J. Kramer/New World Library, 2011.

Millman, Dan. *The Laws of Spirit: Simple, Powerful Truths for Making Life Work*. Tiburon, CA: H. J. Kramer, 1995.

Millman, Dan. *The Life You Were Born to Live: A Guide to Finding Your Life Purpose*. Tiburon, CA: H. J. Kramer, 1993.

Mills, Linde. Linde Mills Art. Knoxville, TN. lindemillsart@gmail.com.

Myss, Caroline. *Anatomy of the Spirit: The Seven Stages of Power and Healing*. New York: Harmony Books, 1996.

Myss, Caroline. *Defy Gravity: Healing Beyond the Bounds of Reason*. Carlsbad, CA: Hay House, 2009.

Myss, Caroline. *Invisible Acts of Power: Channeling Grace in Your Everyday Life*. New York: Free Press, 2004.

Myss, Caroline, and C. Norman Shealy. *The Creation of Health: The Emotional, Psychological, and Spiritual Responses That Promote Health and Healing*. New York: Harmony Books, 1998.

Nerburn, Kent. *Native Echoes: Listening to the Spirit of the Land*. St. Louis Park, MN: Wolf nor Dog Books, 2017.

Nerburn, Kent. *Simple Truths: Clear and Gentle Guidance on the Big Issues in Life*. Novato, CA: New World Library, 1996.

O'Donohue, John. *Anam Cara: A Book of Celtic Wisdom*. New York: HarperCollins, 1998.

O'Donohue, John. *Four Elements: Reflections on Nature*. New York: Harmony Books, 2011.

Remen, Rachel Naomi. *Kitchen Table Wisdom: Stories that Heal*. New York: Riverhead Books, 1996.

Remen, Rachel Naomi. *My Grandfather's Blessings: Stories of Strength, Refuge, and Belonging*. New York: Riverhead Books, 2000.

Rodegast, Pat, and Judith Stanton. *Emmanuel's Book: A Manual for Living Comfortably in the Cosmos*. New York: Bantam Books, 1987.

Schaef, Anne Wilson. *Meditations for Women Who Do Too Much*. New York: Harper & Row, 1990.

Shojai, Pedram. *Inner Alchemy: The Urban Monk's Guide to Happiness, Health, and Vitality*. Boulder, CO: Sounds True, 2018.

St. Cloud, Terri. Bone Sigh Arts. Bone Sigh Arts, 2008. bonesigharts.com.

Teresa, Mother. *A Simple Path. Compiled by Lucinda Vardey*. New York: Ballantine Books, 1995.

Teresa, Mother. *In the Heart of the World: Thoughts, Stories, and Prayers*. Novato, CA: New World Library, 2010.

Teresa, Mother. *No Greater Love*. Edited by Becky Benenate and Joseph Durepos. Novato, CA: New World Library, 1997.

Thoreau, Henry David. *Walden*. Boston, MA: Ticknor and Fields, 1854.

Uktena, Teri. *Akashic Wisdom Newsletter*. Email newsletter.

Virtue, Doreen. *Mornings with the Lord: A Year of Uplifting Devotionals to Start Your Day on the Right Path*. Carlsbad, CA: Hay House, 2017.

Williamson, Marianne. *A Return to Love: Reflections on the Principles of A Course in Miracles*. New York: HarperCollins, 1992.

Williamson, Marianne. *The Gift of Change: Spiritual Guidance for Living Your Best Life*. San Francisco, CA: HarperOne, 2004.

Ywahoo, Dhyani. *108 Quotations: A Treasury of Mystical Wisdom*. CreateSpace Independent Publishing Platform, 2012.

Ywahoo, Dhyani. *Voices of Our Ancestors: Teachings from the Wisdom Fire*. Boston, MA: Shambhala, 1987.

Acknowledgments

My heart speaks with overflowing gratitude.

For my divine calling that energizes and sustains me and urges me forward.

For the angelic realm and my celestial guides whose abundant messages, wisdom, and enlightenment encourage me to translate into words the dimensions of spiritual oneness within me and all of us, in light and love.

For my dear family and friends throughout the world who surround me with pure unconditional love, inner peace, and belief in my becoming and sharing *more*.

For spiritual mentors and energy healers Carolyn A. Jones, the Energy Architect, founder of The Holistic Institute of Wellness and Hilary McCann Crowley, energy medicine practitioner, creator of Good Energy Healing, and author of *The Power of Energy Medicine*. For Candace S. Smith, PhD, RN, for embracing my daily blessings of love that planted a seed, that grew above and below, and flourished into a beautiful Soul Garden of faith, compassion, and hopefulness for all.

For the gifts of the abundant universe. For all who have come before me, are with me, and will find me. For those whose minds are one with all minds in blessed purpose every day. May all be blessed.

About the Author

Sally Gallot-Reeves is a spiritual gardener planting seeds of love. Her life's work as a writer, healer, and life path coach is dedicated to promoting the highest good for all individuals, animals, and nature kingdoms.

Communicating through her writing, she reveals her innermost thoughts and feelings to nurture and guide readers to their own discoveries and awareness. Sally believes compassion, love, and acceptance are the foundation of living in harmony and unity. She credits her years in nursing service to illuminating her heart and mind to the core needs of all people, the sacredness of life, and her dedication to bringing Divine Light and Love into the world.

Her published work includes *The Soul Garden Pathway: Discovery Guide*, a self-help workbook that assists readers in bridging their physical self with spiritual life, and *Between Shifts*, a collection of vignettes of poetry spanning her career in healthcare. Sally's middle grade fiction series Behind the Open Door draws from her background in child behavior, psychology, and nursing to create an exciting, imaginative, mystical world in which children who are feeling misunderstood have a safe place to explore their special abilities.

Born in New England, she resides in New Hampshire, where she continues her literary work and spiritual life creating sanctuary space for all living things.

You may contact her through her websites sallygallotreeves.com and soulgardenpathway.com.

www.ingramcontent.com/pod-product-compliance
Lightning Source LLC
Chambersburg PA
CBHW031022160726
47991CB00005B/1837